WITHDRAWN

Bias in Education

Other Books of Related Interest

Opposing Viewpoints Series
Banned Books
Diversity, Equity, and Inclusion
The Future of Higher Education

At Issue Series
Male Privilege
Partisanship
Student Debt

Current Controversies Series
Freedom of Speech on Campus
Historical Revisionism
Political Correctness

> "Congress shall make no law ... abridging the freedom of speech, or of the press."
>
> *First Amendment to the U.S. Constitution*

The basic foundation of our democracy is the First Amendment guarantee of freedom of expression. The Opposing Viewpoints series is dedicated to the concept of this basic freedom and the idea that it is more important to practice it than to enshrine it.

OPPOSING VIEWPOINTS® SERIES

Bias in Education

Gary Wiener, Book Editor

GREENHAVEN PUBLISHING

Published in 2025 by Greenhaven Publishing, LLC
2544 Clinton Street,
Buffalo NY 14224

Copyright © 2025 by Greenhaven Publishing, LLC

First Edition

All rights reserved. No part of this book may be reproduced in any form without permission in writing from the publisher, except by a reviewer.

Articles in Greenhaven Publishing anthologies are often edited for length to meet page requirements. In addition, original titles of these works are changed to clearly present the main thesis and to explicitly indicate the author's opinion. Every effort is made to ensure that Greenhaven Publishing accurately reflects the original intent of the authors. Every effort has been made to trace the owners of the copyrighted material.

Cover image: Monkey Business Images/Shutterstock.com

Library of Congress CataloginginPublication Data

Names: Wiener, Gary, editor.
Title: Bias in education / Gary Wiener, book editor.
Description: First edition. | Buffalo, NY : Greenhaven Publishing, 2025. | Series: Opposing viewpoints | Includes bibliographical references and index. | Audience: Grades 10-12
Identifiers: LCCN 2024013188 | ISBN 9781534509849 (library binding) | ISBN 9781534509832 (paperback)
Subjects: LCSH: Discrimination in education--United States--Juvenile literature.
Classification: LCC LC212.2 .B54 2025 | DDC 370.80973--dc23/eng/20240416
LC record available at https://lccn.loc.gov/2024013188

Manufactured in the United States of America

Website: http://greenhavenpublishing.com

Contents

The Importance of Opposing Viewpoints	11
Introduction	14

Chapter 1: Are Teachers Biased?

Chapter Preface	18
1. Bias Affects How Teachers Assess Student Work *Wai Yee Amy Wong*	21
2. How Teachers Can Reduce Implicit Bias *Jill Suttie*	25
3. Implicit Bias Has Far-Reaching Effects *Cindy Long*	33
4. Teachers Show Bias Favoring Pupils with Similar Personalities *Peter Tymms*	39
5. Black Students Face Disciplinary Action at a Higher Rate than White Students, but This Can Be Curtailed *Jason Pohl*	43
Periodical and Internet Sources Bibliography	47

Chapter 2: Are School and College Admission Processes Unfairly Biased?

Chapter Preface	50
1. Standardized Testing Has Racist Origins *John Rosales and Tim Walker*	52
2. Standardized Tests Are Not Biased *Adam Tyner*	59
3. The College Admissions Process Is Racist *Elizabeth Redden*	70
4. Ivy League Admissions Purposely Favor the Rich *Matt Bruenig*	81

5. Americans Are Divided About Issues of Race and
   College Admissions   85
   Pew Research Center
Periodical and Internet Sources Bibliography   92

Chapter 3: Is the Current Political Divide Harming Education?
Chapter Preface   95
1. Americans' Opinions About Higher Education
   Are More Divided than Ever   97
   Pew Research Center
2. Brain Drain Is Deepening the Political Divide   107
   Rachel Sheffield and Scott Winship
3. Red and Blue States Battle Over Higher
   Education Policy   112
   John Aubrey Douglass
4. Education Is Inherently Political   123
   Tim Walker
Periodical and Internet Sources Bibliography   128

Chapter 4: Is There Bias in Educational Curricula?
Chapter Preface   131
1. Book Banning Targets Minority Authors   134
   Ariana Figureoa
2. A More Inclusive Curriculum Could Target LGBTQ+
   Bullying in India   139
   Namrata Shokeen and Shivani Chunekar
3. What Critical Race Theory Is, and What It Isn't   144
   Mellissa S. Gordon
4. Conservative Lawmakers Aim to Censor
   School Discussions About Race   150
   Jon Greenberg and Amy Sherman
Periodical and Internet Sources Bibliography   159

For Further Discussion	**161**
Organizations to Contact	**163**
Bibliography of Books	**168**
Index	**170**

Bias in Education

The Importance of Opposing Viewpoints

Perhaps every generation experiences a period in time in which the populace seems especially polarized, starkly divided on the important issues of the day and gravitating toward the far ends of the political spectrum and away from a consensus-facilitating middle ground. The world that today's students are growing up in and that they will soon enter into as active and engaged citizens is deeply fragmented in just this way. Issues relating to terrorism, immigration, women's rights, minority rights, race relations, health care, taxation, wealth and poverty, the environment, policing, military intervention, the proper role of government—in some ways, perennial issues that are freshly and uniquely urgent and vital with each new generation—are currently roiling the world.

If we are to foster a knowledgeable, responsible, active, and engaged citizenry among today's youth, we must provide them with the intellectual, interpretive, and critical-thinking tools and experience necessary to make sense of the world around them and of the all-important debates and arguments that inform it. After all, the outcome of these debates will in large measure determine the future course, prospects, and outcomes of the world and its peoples, particularly its youth. If they are to become successful members of society and productive and informed citizens, students need to learn how to evaluate the strengths and weaknesses of someone else's arguments, how to sift fact from opinion and fallacy, and how to test the relative merits and validity of their own opinions against the known facts and the best possible available information. The landmark series Opposing Viewpoints has been providing students with just such critical-thinking skills and exposure to the debates surrounding society's most urgent contemporary issues for many years, and it continues to serve this essential role with undiminished commitment, care, and rigor.

The key to the series's success in achieving its goal of sharpening students' critical-thinking and analytic skills resides in its title—

Opposing Viewpoints. In every intriguing, compelling, and engaging volume of this series, readers are presented with the widest possible spectrum of distinct viewpoints, expert opinions, and informed argumentation and commentary, supplied by some of today's leading academics, thinkers, analysts, politicians, policy makers, economists, activists, change agents, and advocates. Every opinion and argument anthologized here is presented objectively and accorded respect. There is no editorializing in any introductory text or in the arrangement and order of the pieces. No piece is included as a "straw man," an easy ideological target for cheap point-scoring. As wide and inclusive a range of viewpoints as possible is offered, with no privileging of one particular political ideology or cultural perspective over another. It is left to each individual reader to evaluate the relative merits of each argument—as they see it, and with the use of ever-growing critical-thinking skills—and grapple with their own assumptions, beliefs, and perspectives to determine how convincing or successful any given argument is and how the reader's own stance on the issue may be modified or altered in response to it.

This process is facilitated and supported by volume, chapter, and selection introductions that provide readers with the essential context they need to begin engaging with the spotlighted issues, with the debates surrounding them, and with their own perhaps shifting or nascent opinions on them. In addition, guided reading and discussion questions encourage readers to determine the authors' point of view and purpose, interrogate and analyze the various arguments and their rhetoric and structure, evaluate the arguments' strengths and weaknesses, test their claims against available facts and evidence, judge the validity of the reasoning, and bring into clearer, sharper focus the reader's own beliefs and conclusions and how they may differ from or align with those in the collection or those of their classmates.

Research has shown that reading comprehension skills improve dramatically when students are provided with compelling, intriguing, and relevant "discussable" texts. The subject matter of these collections could not be more compelling, intriguing, or urgently relevant to today's students and the world they are poised to inherit. The anthologized articles and the reading and discussion questions that are included with them also provide the basis for stimulating, lively, and passionate classroom debates. Students who are compelled to anticipate objections to their own argument and identify the flaws in those of an opponent read more carefully, think more critically, and steep themselves in relevant context, facts, and information more thoroughly. In short, using discussable text of the kind provided by every single volume in the Opposing Viewpoints series encourages close reading, facilitates reading comprehension, fosters research, strengthens critical thinking, and greatly enlivens and energizes classroom discussion and participation. The entire learning process is deepened, extended, and strengthened.

For all of these reasons, Opposing Viewpoints continues to be exactly the right resource at exactly the right time—when we most need to provide readers with the critical-thinking tools and skills that will not only serve them well in school but also in their careers and their daily lives as decision-making family members, community members, and citizens. This series encourages respectful engagement with and analysis of opposing viewpoints and fosters a resulting increase in the strength and rigor of one's own opinions and stances. As such, it helps make readers "future ready," and that readiness will pay rich dividends for the readers themselves, for the citizenry, for our society, and for the world at large.

Introduction

> "Children must be taught how to think, not what to think."
>
> –Margaret Mead, American cultural anthropologist

"I don't believe it's humanly possible to be free of bias," says Robin DiAngelo, the author of *White Fragility*. She is correct, of course, though many people would not want to acknowledge it. As author Lillian Hellman once stated, "Nobody outside of a baby carriage or a judge's chamber believes in an unprejudiced point of view." Those who deny bias are either unaware of it or being dishonest with themselves.

So it is no shocking indictment of our way of life to suggest that there is bias in the educational system. In elementary schools, in high schools, and in colleges, examples of bias abound. One can observe them on a daily basis in the classroom, in staff meetings, and in administrative decisions.

How can this be? Conservatives continually attack educators as showing an unmistakably liberal attitude. Teachers, administrators, professors, and deans alike are steeped in sensitivity training (nowadays called Diversity, Equity, Inclusion training), which has exploded since the start of the 2020 Black Lives Matter protests, but which has actually been a feature of teacher and administrator training for decades. The answer goes back to the original premise of this introduction: that it is virtually impossible for a human being to be free of bias.

Bias, in general, is usually defined along these lines: a tendency, inclination, or prejudice toward or against something or someone. Most of those who study bias break it into two main categories:

Introduction

implicit and explicit. According to Professor of Psychology Guy A. Boyson of McKendree University, implicit bias refers to unconscious attitudes, reactions, stereotypes, and categories that affect behavior and understanding. Explicit bias refers to the conscious attitudes, reactions, stereotypes, and categories that affect the way people act. Those with implicit bias may not know or realize how they feel, but the bias may color their actions, causing them to treat some people differently than others without their awareness. Those with explicit bias may say things such as calling a woman a "bimbo" or using the "n-word" or other racist expressions. In both cases, people may not even know why they speak or act with bias.

Given that research suggests that many educators have a liberal political slant, and that schools in general attempt to be welcoming to all students, demonstrations of bias in the classroom are likely to be implicit rather than explicit. Such instances may occur, for example, when a white teacher consistently calls more often on white students to answer questions. The teacher would never admit to believing that white students are more interesting, or have better ideas, or are simply smarter, but these suggestions may be subtly reinforced by the teacher's actions.

Gender bias has long been a form of sometimes implicit, sometimes explicit bias in the schools. It has long been a myth that women performed less well than their male peers in STEM (science, technology, engineering, math) classes. In the past, many women simply did not enroll in STEM courses, accepting society's bias that they would not perform well. For a classic example of how women in a "good ol' boys" discipline were typically treated, one has to look no further than the example of Katherine Johnson, the brilliant mathematician at NASA whose work on orbital mechanics was critical to the success of several early American manned spaceflights. As a Black woman working in the 1960s, Johnson could not have been further away from the stereotype of what a NASA mathematician should have looked like. Known as a "human computer" for her genius with calculations, Johnson was an important contributor to the U.S. space program. Johnson's story is documented in the film and book *Hidden Figures*. The film depicts the many indignities that Johnson had to endure as a Black woman in the space program.

In the 1960s and 1970s, it was not unusual to see STEM courses with enrollments that were 99 percent male. Time has changed those proportions; now, classes in STEM fields, as well as those in more elite professions such as medicine and law, are full of confident young women and other students that do not match the stereotypes who often out-perform the men. But for years, institutional bias held them back.

In *Blink: The Power of Thinking Without Thinking*, Malcolm Gladwell observes that only 3.9 percent of adult men are 6 foot, 2 inches or taller. Yet when it came to company CEOs, roughly a third fell into this group. Gladwell theorized that this could coincide with the unconscious belief that height corresponds with success and power. In schools, it is not uncommon to find that many administrators, such as principals and superintendents, are former physical education teachers. In fact, a 2017 Twitter poll of secondary school teachers (while certainly not a product of rigorous research) found that 67 percent of schools had former physical education teachers among their senior leadership. One might say that these former "gym" teachers are well suited to leadership, as they generally exhibit excellent behavior management strategies and the ability to be well organized as well as to communicate clearly and effectively. But if one were to extrapolate from Gladwell's research, one might also find that there is an unconscious favoritism toward individuals who, oftentimes as former athletes themselves, tend to be taller and more robust in appearance.

Bias in all forms is virtually impossible to eliminate. It is, after all, a part of the human condition. But it can be understood and it can be mitigated. This volume, *Opposing Viewpoints: Bias in Education*, offers a wide range of opinions that present, discuss, and debate the various forms of bias in education, including implicit bias, explicit bias, institutional bias, and many more. Conservative as well as progressive views on educational bias are presented, as well as those in between. Many viewpoints included within offer possible strategies that may be used to acknowledge and ameliorate bias in schools and colleges.

CHAPTER 1

Are Teachers Biased?

Chapter Preface

Because our education system is a reasonably successful, yet imperfect vehicle for educating millions of students a year, and because teachers are often effective, yet imperfect instruments for delivering instruction, and because students are a sometimes successful yet imperfect vessel for receiving instruction, educators are always seeking new ways to improve the system.

In the 1980s, the "shopping mall high school" full of attractive yet unnecessary electives came under scrutiny, and educators attempted to fix the problem of students having too much say in choosing courses. In the 1990s, the teaching of phonics to emerging readers came under fire, and districts initiated "balanced literacy" programs to right the wrongs. In the 2000s, diversity and inclusion programs were instituted across the country to pave the way for more acceptance of underserved minorities and the LGBTQ+ community. In the 2010s, it was educational disciplinary measures that became a target, with many schools instituting "restorative justice" initiatives to serve the needs of recalcitrant learners.

None of these measures, earnestly applied and rigorously followed by educators everywhere, made a significant difference in improving school performance, graduation rates, reading comprehension, etc. And when they didn't work, or did not work up to promised levels, educators moved on to the next educational fad.

It would be inaccurate to simply call the recent concern about teacher bias a fad, however. After all, most if not all teachers do harbor some form of implicit, or even explicit, bias. And it is certainly a noble goal to expose this failing and try to rule it out. But is it a practical one?

In a 2020 paper published in the journal *Educational Researcher*, three Princeton researchers and one from Tufts University, working as a team, found that—shockingly—teachers are people too. As such, they harbor the same biases as their non-teaching fellow citizens. This is a finding that any 11th grader, or teacher for that matter, could have told you. It has long been an open secret that teachers can form opinions that work in favor of some students and against others. When a teacher is not aware of this bias, it is called implicit. When they are fully aware of their preferential or non-preferential treatment, it is called explicit.

Savvy students have long known that getting on a teacher's good side is a sound strategy. Ticking off a teacher is a recipe for disaster. But these examples refer to explicit bias, where teachers know why they feel the way they do about certain students. What is now a point of educational emphasis is implicit bias, which occurs when a teacher is unaware of positive or negative reactions to students of color, or LGBTQ+ students, or students from lower-income families, to cite a few examples.

While it is true that implicit bias is a serious issue about which teachers need to be more aware, it is also true that focusing so intently on teacher bias is something of a diversion. Most teachers want to do the right thing; when alerted to the reality that they are doing the wrong thing, they will generally correct their mistakes.

Most educators are waking up to the reality that implicit bias is real. And correcting this oversight may be good for everyone. But some argue that the educational system has so many more pressing problems that spending energy on seminars exploring teacher bias may not be the best use of their time. As Sarah D. Sparks wrote in *Education Week*, "It's not at all clear from research what kind of anti-bias training works." Perhaps current methods of trying to teach anti-bias are not effective. Or perhaps rooting out implicit bias is difficult to do. As no less an authority than former Supreme Court Justice Ruth Bader Ginsburg has said, "I think unconscious bias is one of the hardest things to get at." Centuries before she made this statement, English writer Jonathan Swift gave a rationale for it: "It is useless to attempt to reason a man out of a thing he was never reasoned into," he said.

All of the anti-bias seminars in the world won't cure the more dire illnesses that affect public education on a daily basis: child poverty, poor parenting, school violence, food insecurity, student mental health. But some argue that this could be an important step in offering equitable opportunities to all students that could have positive lifelong impacts. Others suggest it is far easier to suggest that the microcosmic effects of teacher bias are less of a drag on the school system than it is to deal with the aforementioned ills. Attacking teacher bias won't stop poverty or bigotry. It's just another way of scapegoating teachers for the problems of society.

VIEWPOINT 1

> *"Although teachers are the ones who spend most of the time with students during their learning journey, the reliability of teachers' judgements has sparked heated discussions."*

Bias Affects How Teachers Assess Student Work

Wai Yee Amy Wong

In this viewpoint, Wai Yee Amy Wong cites four factors that may bias how a teacher assesses student work. These four factors include a teacher's beliefs about assessment in general; the teacher's confidence in the assessment process; the teacher's own level of experience; and the teacher's emotions. Teachers should be aware of these biases when grading student work and attempt to be impartial. Research has shown that providing teachers with feedback on their assessment practices is a valuable method of reducing bias. Wai Yee Amy Wong is an associate professor in medical education at the University of East Anglia in Norwich, England.

As you read, consider the following questions:

1. According to this viewpoint, how do teacher's beliefs about assessment affect the way they grade student work?

"Four things that can bias how teachers assess student work", by Wai Yee Amy Wong, The Conversation, July 17, 2020. https://theconversation.com/four-things-that-can-bias-how-teachers-assess-student-work-142135. Licensed under CC BY-ND 4.0 International.

2. How do less experienced teachers fall victim to biased assessment?
3. How can emotions bias a teacher's assessment practices?

The way that teachers assess students has been under scrutiny since the UK government announced that this would be one element of a range of evidence used to replace GCSE and A Level exams this year.

Teacher assessment is a key part of university study, too. University educators play a pivotal role in judging and grading written and non-written tasks in both academic and workplace settings.

Although teachers are the ones who spend most of the time with students during their learning journey, the reliability of teachers' judgements has sparked heated discussions. There are fears that teacher bias regarding students' cultural and linguistic backgrounds could affect student results.

Teachers have to fight against their own subjectivity when giving grades, and being aware of their potential biases is important. My research has identified four factors that can contribute to biases in teachers' judgements.

1. Their Beliefs About Assessment

Teachers who believe the purpose of an assessment is to provide students with an opportunity to learn are likely to be more open to supporting students during the assessment process. For example, they would ask leading questions to help students to cover all the important points in an oral examination.

In contrast, some teachers will believe an assessment is a hurdle, intended to only allow the most competent students to progress. They will usually oppose offering cues to students and adhere strictly to the guidelines.

These different beliefs about assessment influence the level of support provided to students, which may enable some students to be awarded higher marks.

2. Their Confidence in the Process

Well-defined marking criteria – guidelines that clearly describe the key attributes that teachers should follow to assess student performance – are hugely important. They allow teachers to validate their own judgements. Without a set of specific marking criteria, teachers do not feel confident to make pass-or-fail decisions for borderline students.

If teachers believe that the criteria they are given are not up to scratch, they are likely to deviate from them. This means that they may include additional criteria that they consider to be essential, or pay less attention to criteria they perceive as less useful.

This can result in students being assessed using different marking criteria by different teachers, depending on the teachers' own confidence in the materials they have been given.

3. Their Experience

Experience in assessment and expertise in specialty teaching areas influence teacher expectations of student performance. Teachers with years of experience in assessing students usually have a leading role over those with less experience. Less experienced teachers are likely to follow decisions made by experienced teachers, even if they may not always agree with the decisions.

For example, if an experienced teacher regarded a particular assessment as a teaching opportunity for students to learn and therefore did not fail any students, the less experienced teachers are likely to follow their lead.

Another interesting point to note is that when teachers are teaching and subsequently assessing students outside their own specialist area, they may bring with them their own subject-specific expectations. The expectation that students will use a systematic approach to report events for a history class probably isn't quite applicable when marking a creative essay in English.

4. Their Emotions

Emotion plays a key part in teaching and learning. In face-to-face performance assessment, teachers could become frustrated if they perceive the student, for whatever reason, as not being respectful of the examination process. These frustrations might distort teachers' judgements – the perceived poor behavior could overshadow the ability demonstrated by the student.

In fact, teacher emotion is an underlying factor which affects all the above interrelated factors. Teacher emotion will influence how they use the marking criteria, which also depends on their beliefs about the purpose of the assessment.

While teacher subjectivity might seem worrying, the picture is not all gloomy. The current situation creates an opportunity to rethink teacher assessment as a professional practice. We can consider how it can be best combined with other evidence to provide students with accurate and credible assessment of their ability.

An understanding of the above four factors helps to increase teachers' awareness of their own biases when marking student performance. Research showed that providing teachers with feedback on their assessment practice might help them to realise their marking behaviour.

The feedback creates a learning opportunity for teachers to formally review and reflect on their marking behaviour, and potentially make changes. After all, everyone appreciates feedback about their work if it is constructive and means well.

VIEWPOINT

> "Providing the background information on the child increased the severity of suggested disciplinary actions when the race of the teacher didn't match that of the child, supporting the idea that we are more inclined to punish those who look different from us."

How Teachers Can Reduce Implicit Bias
Jill Suttie

Jill Suttie begins this viewpoint by providing examples of implicit bias in the classroom relating to race. Such bias on the part of the teacher may have devastating effects, she writes. But teachers can learn to combat their implicit biases. A first step is admitting that we are all human and that implicit bias exists. Teachers should also learn about the lives of students and show that they care. Suttie further suggests teachers should practice mindfulness and seek out and form friendships with people who are different from themselves. Jill Suttie is the Greater Good's former book review editor and now serves as a staff writer and contributing editor for the online magazine. She received her PhD in psychology from the University of San Francisco and was a psychologist in private practice before coming to Greater Good.

"Four Ways Teachers Can Reduce Implicit Bias," by Jill Suttie, The Greater Good Science Center at the University of California, Berkeley, October 28, 2016. Reprinted by permission.

Bias in Education

As you read, consider the following questions:

1. How does the belief that one is "colorblind" often lead to increased racial bias, according to Suttie?
2. How does the practice of mindfulness help teachers confront their implicit bias?
3. What can school districts do to reduce bias among their teachers?

A friend of mine recently told me about an incident involving students at Berkeley High School. On the first day of classes, African American juniors and seniors were being asked by their honors course teacher to show him their schedule when they entered the classroom. The teacher, who was white, apparently assumed the Black students were lost and in the wrong room, and his gesture made them feel unwelcome and humiliated.

This is an example of implicit bias—a behavior that arises from subconscious associations, which may even contradict someone's explicit values. Implicit racial bias plays a role in many classrooms and schools with potentially devastating effects. In one recent experiment with preschool teachers, researchers found that when teachers were primed to look for behavioral problems while watching a classroom video with Black and white children (none of whom were misbehaving), teachers gazed much longer at Black children than white children, as if anticipating the behavioral problems would come from the Black children.

In another experiment from the same study, teachers read a vignette about a behavioral problem with a preschooler randomly identified as a Black boy, Black girl, white boy, or white girl, and then were given details about the child's background or not. Providing the background information on the child increased the severity of suggested disciplinary actions when the race of the teacher didn't match that of the child, supporting the idea that we are more inclined to punish those who look different from us.

In fact, disciplinary actions are more likely to be perpetuated against African Americans—boys and girls alike—than any other group of students, regardless of the infraction. And while it's understandable that teachers would want to prevent disruptions in the classrooms and take actions to avoid them, some seem to have little idea of how to do that without turning to ingrained biases.

Of course, teachers are not alone in having racial biases. Their behavior reflects how social messages are hard to escape, even for people of color. But studies like these show how racial disparities can be perpetuated in classrooms, too. If left unchecked, this kind of biased treatment can haunt a student well into elementary school and beyond, making the promise of "schools as the great social equalizers" a false one.

The good news is that teachers *can* learn to combat their prejudice, even the implicit kind, if they become more aware of it and take steps to actively fight it in themselves. Here are some of the ways that might help educators treat all of their students with dignity and care.

1. Cultivate Awareness of Their Biases

Teachers are human and therefore influenced by psychological biases, like the fundamental attribution error, when we assume that others who behave in a certain way do so because of their character (a fixed trait) rather than in response to environmental circumstances. In-group bias leads us to assign positive characteristics and motivations to people who are similar to us.

Biases like these are natural, used as cognitive shorthand for making quick social judgments in ambiguous situations, especially those involving people from unfamiliar ethnic or social groups. They become a problem when we're not aware of their impact on other people. And if we're part of a majority group with more social, economic, or political power than a minority one, then accumulated unconscious bias can be extremely destructive, limiting the life opportunities and hurting the well-being of the minority group.

Many researchers believe that becoming more aware of our biases can help us improve our interactions with others, decrease our sense of unease in interracial contexts, and make better decisions. Though most of this research has been done with other professional groups or the general public, the same lessons are likely to apply to teachers.

However, many teachers feel pressures not to cop to those biases, perhaps out of fear they will be accused of racism. This leaves them blind to the ways that biases work at an unconscious level. Pretending to be colorblind is *not* helpful and in fact adhering to a color-blind philosophy has been shown to increase implicit bias, at least in college students. Admitting that we are all subject to biases creates a safer space to examine them more carefully and to take steps to fight them.

2. Work to Increase Empathy and Empathic Communication

Empathy—the ability to understand another's perspective and emotions—is important in all human social encounters, including teaching. Yet, often teachers have little understanding of the communities where their students live and have trouble understanding their perspectives, leading them to treat these students more harshly.

One solution: learning about the lives of students and showing that you care. At least one study has found that actively trying to take the perspective of another person—as opposed to trying to be "objective"—increased one's ability to not fall prey to stereotypical views of others. Actively inducing empathy for another person has been tied to a willingness to consider environmental circumstances more closely when handing out punishments for misbehavior. And, one recent study has found that training teachers in empathy cut down student suspension rates in half.

Though perhaps more research has been done on empathy in other professionals (such as physicians and police officers), teachers may want to take note of the ways that they have learned to increase their empathy through a combination of stress reduction, learning how to manage difficult emotions, and practicing empathic communication. Treating students with kindness and consideration is a sure way to bring out kindness in them too.

3. Practice Mindfulness and Loving-Kindness

Mindfulness practices—such as paying attention in a nonjudgmental way to one's breath or other sensations—has been shown to decrease stress in teachers, which can indirectly have an effect on reducing bias. But according to some research, mindfulness may also have a direct effect on bias reduction as well.

In one study, young white participants who listened to a 10-minute audiotape with instructions in mindfulness showed less implicit bias towards Blacks and older people than those who listened to a 10-minute discussion of nature. This suggests that nonjudgmental awareness, even when not specifically focused on reducing prejudice, can help reduce unconscious biases.

Loving-kindness meditation—a practice that involves consciously sending out compassionate thoughts toward others—may also help. In a recent study, the random assignment of a short-term loving-kindness meditation reduced implicit bias toward a targeted group, though it didn't decrease implicit bias for other groups not targeted by the meditation.

4. Develop Cross-Group Friendships in Their Own Lives

While it's important to take steps in the classroom, the relationships we form outside of the classroom can also have an impact on bias.

Cross-group friendships have been shown in several studies to decrease stress in intergroup situations, to decrease prejudice toward outgroup members, and to decrease one's preference for social hierarchy or domination over lower-status groups. These findings alone might encourage teachers to seek out cross-group friendships in their lives so that they can be more receptive to the diverse students they find in their classrooms.

How Teachers Can Combat Implicit Bias

Biases can be either conscious or unconscious and can motivate people to act favorably or unfavorably towards groups of people:
- Explicit bias (or conscious bias) refers to when a person is aware of holding stereotypes about social groups.
- Implicit bias (or hidden bias or unconscious bias) refers to when a person is not aware of holding explicit stereotypes of social groups.

Everyone has implicit biases. Jennifer L. Eberhardt, in *Biased: Uncovering the Hidden Prejudice That Shapes What We see, Think, and Do* (2019) explains implicit bias as "a kind of distorting lens that's a product of both the architecture of our brain and the disparities in our society." People develop ideas about many characteristics, including race, weight, ethnic origin, accent, religion, gender, and disability based on their past experiences, geographical location, popular culture, etc. Those ideas have the "power to power to bias our perception, our attention, our memory, and our actions—all despite our conscious awareness or deliberate intentions."

Mahzarin R. Banaji and Anthony G. Greenwald (2013) emphasize the hidden nature of implicit biases. They explain how hidden biases can plant "mindbugs," or "ingrained habits of thought that lead to errors in how we perceive, remember, reason, and make decisions." Those habits come from unrecognized feelings and beliefs about social groups.

In other words, people have to learn about their implicit biases and work to combat them.

Combating Bias

These are some strategies for combating bias in your teaching:

1. Identify your biases. Take an online self-assessment to help identify your biases through Harvard's Project Implicit.
2. Consider using grading and assessment techniques that may help mitigate bias. Some examples include blind marking and contract grading. In Labor-Based Grading Contracts, Asao B. Inoue argues for the use of labor-based grading contracts.

3. Diversify your curriculum. Doing so may help to counter stereotypes.
4. Facilitate equitable participation during class activities and discussions.
5. Ask for feedback from your peers by asking a colleague to observe your course.

"Implicit Bias," DePaul University.

Another reason for teachers to consider developing cross-group friendships is that they may influence their students to do the same. When people see cross-group friendships working out in positive ways, they tend to be more willing to engage in cross-group friendships themselves.

In addition, positive cross-group friendships can have contagion effects in other people within social groups, turning whole communities into warmer, more receptive spaces for cross-group interactions. All of this bodes well for teachers role-modeling the kind of behavior they want to see in their students.

Of course, this doesn't necessarily mean teachers should indiscriminately approach someone just because they are from a different racial group. Instead, teachers can reach out to colleagues at work, or get involved in activities or perhaps attend events where people with different backgrounds and perspectives come together for a common cause. Developing friendships can be one of the best ways to break down barriers of prejudice, and it's more easily done when people have some common interests.

Is this a lot to ask, given all the burdens our society heaps on teachers? Perhaps. Teachers should get more support than they do, and, ideally, school districts should make reducing implicit bias a priority backed up with money, policy, and training. Individual teachers can only do so much.

Luckily, the teaching profession tends to attract altruists who *want* to teach in a way that helps their students. By working at countering implicit bias in themselves, they can truly make a difference in the lives of their students, making them feel safe, cared for, and welcome in the classroom.

VIEWPOINT 3

> *"Although we strive to be fair and impartial as educators, biases creep in—an uncomfortable truth for many white educators who consider themselves to be progressive, open-minded, and socially conscious and who have fought hard to battle racism in their schools and communities."*

Implicit Bias Has Far-Reaching Effects

Cindy Long

In this viewpoint, Cindy Long cites the example of a Black high school student whom an educator erroneously believed to be a special education student based simply on her race. This and other implicit biases among educators have far-reaching effects on student behavior and academic success that educators may not be aware of. Long provides a couple of exercises designed to target implicit bias. But one of the most effective ways to counter such bias, she concludes, is simply by accepting that bias exists and discussing how it manifests and its implications. Cindy Long is a senior writer and media specialist at the National Education Association.

"The Far-Reaching Effects of Implicit Bias in the Classroom," by Cindy Long, National Education Association, January 26, 2016. Reprinted by permission.

But just as implicit biases are learned, new mental associations can be acquired to replace damaging biases. The first step is awareness, says Kevin Teeley, an NEA diversity trainer from Redmond, Washington. That awareness arises from honest and thoughtful reflection.

"NEA's diversity training provides our members with reflective experiences in a safe environment, so that people get to those big 'aha' moments, where they'll often say, 'I never realized this about myself,' " Teeley says. "When you lead people to draw their own conclusions rather than lecturing them on how bad they are and that they have racist behaviors, they'll step back and be able to recognize their own biases."

One of the most effective awareness-raising exercises in the program is called "memory sharing." Participants close their eyes and think about their earliest experience with someone from a different race. Who was there? What happened? What were their reflections on this? When they think about their first experience with someone from a different religion, sexual orientation, or disability?

"It's extraordinarily powerful in how those early experiences impact how they think today," says Teeley. "Some people cry and get very emotional, and we see quite a few 'ahas,' which often come after others share their perspectives."

Teeley says training is key to helping us overcome our biases, but it needs to be ongoing. "You can't do it once and expect it to stick," he says.

This is true especially of "hot button" issues, another exercise in which the trainers point out some hot button issues educators inadvertently hit with comments that they don't intend to be offensive.

For example, many people talk about the gay lifestyle, as if people who are gay live a different lifestyle and have "disco balls hanging in their living rooms," Teeley says.

Sometimes people will touch on hot button issues when they call on female students to help at the front of the class. "Will you be my lovely assistant?" Or "You can be my Vanna White."

"It's surprisingly common," Teeley says, "And it puts the female in a very superficial role. What message does that send to the girls in the class? To all the students in the class?"

Sometimes, Teeley says, educators think they're saying something positive, like when they make racial statements in the affirmative. "The Asain kids really good at math," or "We have a lot of Asian kids in our community so we have really great test scores." It's a racial bias based on the assumption that Asians are always good students, particularly in math and science.

He says people are more guarded when it comes to African American issues, but he recalls one participant say, "well, you know those people want to live in that section of town because that's where they feel most at home and comfortable."

After he pointed out that referring to a group as "those people" is demeaning, participants arrived at yet another "aha moment."

But there's a long way to go and Teeley wishes every educator would seek out diversity training and keep at it.

"There are some who say racism is no longer a problem—they point to Obama and say, 'We have a Black president! We must be post-racial.' But when you look at Ferguson and Baltimore and all the other headlines, there is clear evidence that racism is alive and well," Teeley says.

It's imperative that educators continue to work on removing their biases, he says, because implicit bias has a major impact in a student's ability to learn and feel valued.

"Everyone wants to feel like they belong, that they are important and valued. All students need to feel safe and important, that their contributions are appreciated and that they add to the greater good of the entire classroom experience," Teeley says. "If they don't feel that, they'll feel diminished worth, they'll be less likely to participate, work hard, or be engaged or successful."

Bias in Education

Adia Brown has felt that she contributes to her classroom's experience, and that her teachers, especially her AP teachers, hold everyone to the same standards, but she is usually one of only a few minorities in the classes and she senses that some educators "are surprised when I or other minority students do well."

She acknowledges that she might be wrong—perhaps there's an implicit bias at play—but she thinks the best way to address it is to talk about it.

"I think we can help eliminate bias by having a conversation," Brown says. "I think that sometimes we try to avoid the conversation for fear of awkwardness, but I think a simple conversation can be powerful and effective."

VIEWPOINT 4

> "But for every judgment there is baggage: girls are better at reading, Asians are better at math, older people don't learn languages as quickly, and so on. While each of these generalizations have some validity, they are based on differences in very large samples and they are not valuable when we are dealing with individuals."

Teachers Show Bias Favoring Pupils with Similar Personalities

Peter Tymms

In this viewpoint, Peter Tymms takes an unusual angle when it comes to teacher assessment of students. Tymms writes about studies indicating that teachers will favor students who have similar personalities to themselves when judging their work. Regardless of other factors, the more similar the personalities of students are to their teacher's, the more likely it is that the teacher will score them highly when it comes to subjective measures. Nevertheless, these studies don't suggest that teacher judgments should be abandoned altogether, but that teachers need to be aware of their biases when scoring student work. Peter Tymms is a director in the School of Education at Durham University in England. His main research

"Teachers show bias to pupils who share their personality," by Peter Tymms, The Conversation, February 25, 2015. https://theconversation.com/teachers-show-bias-to-pupils-who-share-their-personality-38018. Licensed under CC BY-ND 4.0 International.

Bias in Education

interests include monitoring, assessment, performance indicators, ADHD, reading, and research methodology.

As you read, consider the following questions:

1. What personality traits encompass "the big five," according to Tymms?
2. What stereotypes does Tymms cite regarding types of students?
3. What solutions does Tymms suggest in concluding his viewpoint?

The more similar the personalities of teachers and their pupils, the more likely the teachers are to grade them highly, according to new research from Germany. The findings again open up the debate around the subtle biases teachers have about their pupils and how important it is to try and minimize their impact on children's progress through school.

Tobias Rausch from the University of Bamberg in Germany and his colleagues carried out an investigation with Grade 8 classes in Germany. First, they asked 94 teachers to rate their 293 pupils, aged 13 to 14, on reading comprehension and some areas of mathematics using a scale from one (very weak) to five (very good). The teachers were then asked to estimate if each pupil would get specific tasks in reading and mathematics correct or not. Both the teachers and pupils also then completed a short personality questionnaire measuring the "big five" dimensions of personality: extraversion, agreeableness, conscientiousness, openness, and neuroticism. Finally the pupils were given tests of mathematics and reading.

Personality Counts

The researchers expected, as others have found, that they would find bias in the teachers' judgments. But they reasoned that the more similar the personalities of teachers and pupils, the more the teachers would be in tune with the pupils and the higher the teachers would rate the pupils' work.

Their analysis did show a significant link between the overall ratings teachers gave to each pupil and their actual test scores. But they discovered that the degree of similarity between pairs of teachers and pupils helped to explain where teachers made overall judments about pupils' reading and math ability that were over and above the test scores. But, as Rausch and his colleagues had predicted, personality similarity did not add to teachers' ratings of competence on specific tasks. This could be because global judgments tend to bring in extraneous factors such as personality whereas the specific judgments allow less room for maneuvering.

Other researchers in the UK have been looking at the issue of teacher bias in recent years. Education researcher Wynne Harlen has been a great supporter of the view that we should trust and reply on teacher judgment. But it is to her credit that in 2005 she took a careful look at research into the area and wrote that "there was evidence of low reliability and bias in teachers' judgments".

In 2009, researchers Simon Burgess and Ellen Greaves also looked at teacher judgments at the end of Key Stage 2 in relation to ethnic minorities. They concluded:

> We find evidence that some ethnic groups are systematically "under-assessed" relative to their white peers, while some are "over-assessed."

Aware of Our Leanings

There are several implications of these findings for our education systems—the most obvious being that we should all aim to be aware of our biases and make corrections. This might be harder than it seems, as we make sense of the world around us by trying to simplify it and by categorizing. As soon as we meet someone, we notice gender, age, and ethnicity. When we start interacting with them, we pick up more information which helps us assess and categorize that person. This is essential: by understanding people we can interact with them better and, as teachers, educate them better.

But for every judgment there is baggage: girls are better at reading, Asians are better at math, older people don't learn languages as quickly, and so on. While each of these generalizations have some validity, they are based on differences in very large samples and they are not valuable when we are dealing with individuals.

But this does not mean we should discard teacher judgment altogether. Judgment lies at the heart of good teaching and I would venture to suggest that the very best teachers are best at judging their students. For some things such as attentiveness, there is no alternative—they must be assessed by judgment.

Use Judgment Appropriately

Other things need to be assessed by judgment but in a controlled way. Essay writing is a case in point: the length of the essay and the title can be controlled while the marking can be constrained to make it as fair as possible. One important step, for high-stakes exams, is to ensure that the marker is "blind" to any characteristic of the writer. This means substituting names for ID numbers as well as hiding the school name. Together they might give indications of sex, ethnicity, religious persuasion, and social class.

There is an argument that even judgment-free tests are also biased. But modern psychometric tests have developed techniques designed to identify biased items and a well-constructed test should have had bias reduced to a minimum.

The inevitable bias of us all and the need to use judgments for some but not all assessments means that a one-size-fits-all solution to assessment would be wrong. I believe it would be unethical to insist, as some do, that young children must only be assessed by observation. We need to choose the mode of assessment to fit the task in hand. When life-changing human judgments are needed, they need to come from several independent professionals ideally with similar personality, sex, and ethnicity to the person being judged.

VIEWPOINT 5

> *"If principals or teachers know by Halloween in any given year these students are facing this very heightened risk of being kicked out of school, or in which schools these students face the highest risk, we can get in there and do something about it, as opposed to letting it fester."*

Black Students Face Disciplinary Action at a Higher Rate than White Students, but This Can Be Curtailed

Jason Pohl

Jason Pohl writes about the inequities in student discipline in this viewpoint. According to a University of California, Berkeley study, Pohl asserts that student suspensions can be predicted based on the time of year and proximity to various school holidays. Knowing this information, the study's authors suggest, can cut discipline and suspension rates, particularly for Black students. Doing a specific intervention at a time when disciplinary actions are scheduled to jump, the authors suggest, would cut suspension rates and save money. Furthermore, this would offer Black students a more positive and equitable educational experience. Jason Pohl writes about science and media relations. He was formerly an investigative reporter at the Sacramento Bee, *covering criminal justice and government accountability.*

"School discipline can be predicted, new research says. Is it preventable?," by Jason Pohl, Berkeley News, April 17, 2023. Reprinted by permission.

"It is incredibly important, useful and valuable to know we should do a specific type of intervention at a specific point in the year based on the real-time data. That's where we're going to get the biggest bang for our buck," Okonofua said. "If we can be more cost-efficient, everybody wins."

Okonofua's co-authors — Sean Darling-Hammond of UCLA, Michael Ruiz of UC Berkeley, and Jennifer L. Eberhardt of Stanford University — also published a short video that uses beeping tones to illustrate discipline disparities between Black and white students. The anxiety-inducing tones are meant to simulate how stressful school can be when students are witnessing increasing discipline.

Okonofua likened school discipline tracking tools to an athlete's heart rate monitor at the gym. Rather than simply estimating how hard a workout was, real-time data can be more useful.

"The more data we have, the more we know," Okonofua said. "And the more we know, the more we can do."

The study shows how important it is for districts to create systems for teachers to regularly monitor school discipline, he said. Policy leaders should likewise take note as they write policies and dedicate funding meant to curb discipline, alleviate disparities, and minimize disruption.

"It's important to think about each data point. That's a whole story," said Okonofua, reflecting on discipline's lasting effects on both the student in trouble and classmates witnessing the punishment. "I hope we can do as much as possible going forward to just keep in mind that each one of these data points is a whole life."

Periodical and Internet Sources Bibliography

The following articles have been selected to supplement the diverse views presented in this chapter.

"Teacher Bias by the Numbers," *Unbound Ed*, July 24, 2020. https://www.unbounded.org/blog/teacher-bias-by-the-numbers.

Kavita Anand, "The myth of the unbiased teacher," *TeacherPlus*, August 2023. https://www.teacherplus.org/the-myth-of-the-unbiased-teacher/.

Tasminda K. Dhaliwal, Mark J. Chin, Virginia S. Lovison, and David M. Quinn, "Educator bias is associated with racial disparities in student achievement and discipline," Brookings, July 20, 2020. https://www.brookings.edu/articles/educator-bias-is-associated-with-racial-disparities-in-student-achievement-and-discipline/.

Colleen Flaherty, "The Skinny on Teaching Evals and Bias," *Inside Higher Ed*, February 16, 2021. https://www.insidehighered.com/news/2021/02/17/whats-really-going-respect-bias-and-teaching-evals.

Ajmel Quereshi and Jason Okonofua, "Locked Out of the Classroom: How Implicit Bias Contributes to Disparities in School Discipline," Legal Defense Fund, 2017-2018. https://www.naacpldf.org/wp-content/uploads/LDF_Bias_Report_WEB-2.pdf.

David M. Quinn, "Experimental Evidence on Teachers' Racial Bias in Student Evaluation: The Role of Grading Scales," Harvard University, 2020. https://scholar.harvard.edu/files/dmq/files/quinn-racial-bias-grading-eepa-2020.pdf.

Tiara Smith and Jennifer Pham, "Understanding Teacher Bias: Acknowledging the Impact of Unconscious Bias," Learning A-Z. https://www.learninga-z.com/site/resources/breakroom-blog/understanding-teacher-bias.

Sarah D. Sparks, "Training Bias Out of Teachers: Research Shows Little Promise So Far," *Education Week*, November 17, 2020. https://www.edweek.org/leadership/training-bias-out-of-teachers-research-shows-little-promise-so-far/2020/11 .

Cheryl Staats, "Understanding Implicit Bias: What Educators Should Know," *American Educator*, Winter 2015–2016. https://www.aft.org/sites/default/files/ae_winter2015staats.pdf.

Jordan G. Starck, Travis Riddle, Stacey Sinclair, and Natasha Warikoo, "Teachers are people too: Racial bias among American educators," Brookings, July 13, 2020. https://www.brookings.edu/articles/teachers-are-people-too-racial-bias-among-american-educators/.

Madeline Will, "Teachers Are as Racially Biased as Everybody Else, Study Shows," *Education Week*, June 9, 2020. https://www.edweek.org/teaching-learning/teachers-are-as-racially-biased-as-everybody-else-study-shows/2020/06.

OPPOSING VIEWPOINTS® SERIES

CHAPTER 2

Are School and College Admissions Processes Unfairly Biased?

Chapter Preface

In the late 20th century, college entrance exams came under fire, with critics arguing that they were racially and socio-economically biased. But these accusations did not result in changes until fairly recently, when a number of high-profile universities moved to a test-optional admissions policy in an effort to be—or at least seem to be—more fair.

But experts now say that the elimination of mandatory standardized testing requirements may not move the needle much when it comes to combating systemic bias in college acceptances. The rich will still get into prestigious colleges at a far higher rate than their less affluent counterparts.

Systemic bias occurs when institutional practices favor specific social groups, while other groups experience disadvantages. Systemic bias may not occur due to prejudice or discrimination but instead from the following of established rules and norms by the majority.

The college admissions process—especially for elite and prestigious schools—has long been an example of systemic bias. Making the SAT and ACT college entrance examinations optional may not change that reality. In fact, if experts are to be believed, optional testing may actually favor the wealthy. The elimination of affirmative action will also help maintain the status quo for the wealthy in education.

Why is this? Simply put, the wealthy will always have an advantage when it comes to college admissions, as they do in just about everything else. Recently, the "Varsity Blues" scandal provided an example of this phenomenon. The scandal involved wealthy parents paying to have surrogates take entrance exams for their college-bound children. College coaches were bribed to accept these applicants for their intercollegiate sports teams as a way of getting a student's foot in the door of prestigious colleges.

A lot of people went to prison or paid substantial fines when the cheating scandal was exposed in 2019.

But wealthy parents do not have to use illegal means to game the college admissions system. Effective legal methods of greasing the college entrance system wheels have become more and more common. Companies such as Command Education, Ivy Coach, Ivy Wise, and numerous others will go to extraordinary lengths to ensure that the children of wealthy parents get admitted to prestigious institutions of higher learning.

In a *New York Magazine* article from January 2024 entitled "Inventing the Perfect College Applicant," writer Caitlin Moscatello demonstrated just how far wealthy New Yorkers will go to assure their children a ticket to the Ivy League. Moscatello interviewed Christopher Rim, founder and CEO of Command Education. Rim is a 28-year-old Yale graduate who is now a multi-millionaire. His company benefits from the fact that wealthy parents will pay up to $120,000 a year to have their children shepherded through the college admissions process. Rim provides them with personal counselors, who themselves can make up to $200,000 a year, and who will guide the students—sometimes as young as seventh graders—through every step of the lead-up to college. According to Moscatello, this includes a "'personalized, white glove' service, through which Command employees do everything from curating students' extracurriculars to helping them land summer internships, craft essays, and manage their course loads with the single goal of getting them in."

Such advantages are totally unheard of in the world of middle-class folks, to say nothing of the even less privileged. But it is the reality of the college admissions racket in the 21st century.

VIEWPOINT 1

> "Since their inception almost a century ago, the tests have been instruments of racism and a biased system. Decades of research demonstrate that Black, Latin(o/a/x), and Native students, as well as students from some Asian groups, experience bias from standardized tests administered from early childhood through college."

Standardized Testing Has Racist Origins

John Rosales and Tim Walker

John Rosales and Tim Walker write about the use of standardized tests in the aftermath of the COVID pandemic. Such tests, they contend, have never been an accurate measure of student learning. The tests are biased, and, as such, are an effective "weapon" in keeping minority students out of prestigious colleges. Instead, as Rosales and Walker write, there is a correlation between standardized test scores and familial wealth. For Rosales and Walker, standardized tests were originally developed to promote and maintain a system where those with money have an advantage, and minority and less affluent students are penalized. John Rosales and Tim Walker write for NEA Today, *the publication of the National Education Association.*

"The Racist Beginnings of Standardized Testing", by John Rosales and Tim Walker, National Education Association, March 20, 2021. Reprinted by permission.

Are School and College Admissions Processes Unfairly Biased?

As you read, consider the following questions:

1. Why, according to Rosales and Walker, are standardized tests biased?
2. What is the racist history of standardized tests, according to this viewpoint?
3. According to the authors, where should the focus be for testing in the future?

As many students return to in-person learning for the first time in almost a year, states and school districts are also beginning to gear up for statewide standardized testing, as required by the U.S. Department of Education (ED).

In April 2020, as the pandemic engulfed the nation and forced schools to close, the department granted a "blanket waiver" to every state to skip mandated statewide testing for 2019–20. Last month, however, ED officials announced it was mandating schools to administer some form of statewide assessment for 2020–21.

Educators across the country criticized the decision, saying the idea that students should be forced to take any sort of standardized test this year is incomprehensible. The priority right now should be on strengthening instruction and support for students and families in communities most traumatized by the impact of the coronavirus.

Many of these same communities have suffered the most from high-stakes testing. Since their inception almost a century ago, the tests have been instruments of racism and a biased system. Decades of research demonstrate that Black, Latin(o/a/x), and Native students, as well as students from some Asian groups, experience bias from standardized tests administered from early childhood through college.

"We still think there's something wrong with the kids rather than recognizing their something wrong with the tests," Ibram X. Kendi of the Antiracist Research & Policy Center at Boston University and author of *How to Be an Antiracist* said in October 2020. "Standardized tests have become the most effective racist

Bias in Education

weapon ever devised to objectively degrade Black and brown minds and legally exclude their bodies from prestigious schools."

Yet some organizations insist on *more* testing, arguing that the data will expose the gaps where support and resources should be directed.

Standardized tests, however, have never been accurate and reliable measures of student learning.

"While much has been said about the racial achievement gap as a civil rights issue, more attention needs to be paid to the measurement tools used to define that gap," explains Young Wan Choi, manager of performance assessments for the Oakland Unified school District in Oakland, CA. "Education reformists, civil rights organizations, and all who are concerned with racial justice in education need to advocate for assessment tools that don't replicate racial and economic inequality."

Testing Pioneer—and Eugenicist

"To tell the truth about standardized tests," Kendi said, "is to tell the story of the eugenicists who created and popularized these tests in the United States more than a century ago."

As the U.S. absorbed millions of immigrants from Europe beginning in the 19th century, the day's leading social scientists, many of them white Anglo-Saxon Protestants, were concerned by the infiltration of non-whites into the nation's public schools.

In his 1923 book, *A Study of American Intelligence*, psychologist and eugenicist Carl Brigham wrote that African Americans were on the low end of the racial, ethnic, and/or cultural spectrum. Testing, he believed, showed the superiority of "the Nordic race group" and warned of the "promiscuous intermingling" of new immigrants in the American gene pool.

Furthermore, the education system he argued was in decline and "will proceed with an accelerating rate as the racial mixture becomes more and more extensive."

Brigham had helped to develop aptitude tests for the U.S. Army during World War I and—commissioned by the College Board

—was influential in the development of the Scholastic Aptitude Test (SAT). At the time, he and other social scientists considered the SAT a new psychological test and a supplement to existing college board exams.

The SAT debuted in 1926, joined by the ACT (American College Testing) in the 1950s. By the 21st century, the SAT and ACT were just part of a barrage of tests students may face before reaching college. The College Board also offers SAT II tests, designed for individual subjects ranging from biology to geography.

Entrenched in Schools

Brigham's Ph.D. dissertation, written in 1916, "Variable Factors in the Binet Tests," analyzed the work of the French psychologist Alfred Binet, who developed intelligence tests as diagnostic tools to detect learning disabilities. The Stanford psychologist Lewis Terman relied on Binet's work to produce today's standard IQ test, the Stanford-Binet Intelligence Tests.

During World War I, standardized tests helped place 1.5 million soldiers in units segregated by race and by test scores. The tests were scientific yet they remained deeply biased, according to researchers and media reports.

In 1917, Terman and a group of colleagues were recruited by the American Psychological Association to help the U.S. Army develop group intelligence tests and a group intelligence scale. Army testing during World War I ignited the most rapid expansion of the school testing movement.

By 1918, there were more than 100 standardized tests, developed by different researchers to measure achievement in the principal elementary and secondary school subjects. The U.S. Bureau of Education reported in 1925 that intelligence and achievement tests were increasingly used to classify students at all levels.

The first SAT was administered in 1926 to more than 8,000 students, 40 percent of them female. The original test lasted 90 minutes and consisted of 315 questions focused on vocabulary and basic math.

"Unlike the college boards, the SAT is designed primarily to assess aptitude for learning rather than mastery of subjects already learned," according to Erik Jacobsen, a New Jersey writer and math-physics teacher based at Newark Academy in Livingston, N.J. "For some college officials, an aptitude test, which is presumed to measure intelligence, is appealing since at this time (1926) intelligence and ethnic origin are thought to be connected, and therefore the results of such a test could be used to limit the admissions of particularly undesirable ethnicities."

By 1930, multiple-choice tests were firmly entrenched in U.S. schools. The rapid spread of the SAT sparked debate along two lines. Some critics viewed the multiple-choice format as encouraging memorization and guessing. Others examined the content of the questions and reached the conclusion that the tests were racist.

Eventually, Brigham adapted the army test for use in college admissions, and his work began to interest interested administrators at Harvard University. Starting in 1934, Harvard adopted the SAT to select scholarship recipients at the school. Many institutions of higher learning soon followed suit.

The Triumph of Pseudo-Science

In his essay "The Racist Origins of the SAT," Gil Troy calls Brigham a "Pilgrim-pedigreed, eugenics-blinded bigot." Eugenics is often defined as the science of improving a human population by controlled breeding to increase the occurrence of desirable heritable characteristics. It was developed by Francis Galton as a method of improving the human race. Only after the perversion of its doctrines by the Nazis in World War II was the theory dismissed.

"All-American decency and idealism coexisted uncomfortably with these scientists' equally American racism and closemindedness," Troy writes.

Binet, Terman, and Brigham stood at the intersection of powerful intellectual, ideological, and political trends a century ago when the Age of Science and standardization began, according to Troy.

"In (those) consensus-seeking times, scientists became obsessed with deviations and handicaps, both physical and intellectual," Troy states. "And many social scientists, misapplying Charles Darwin's evolving evolutionary science, and eugenics' pseudo-science, worried about maintaining white purity."

Decades of Racial Bias

By the 1950s and 1960s, top U.S. universities were talent-searching for the "brainy kids," regardless of ethnicity, states Jerome Karabel in "The Chosen: The Hidden History of Admission and Exclusion at Harvard, Yale, and Princeton."

This dictum among universities to identify the brightest students as reflected by test scores did not bode well for students from communities of color, who were—as a result of widespread bias in testing—disproportionately failing state or local high school graduation exams, according to the National Center for Fair and Open Testing (FairTest).

According to Fair Test, on average, students of color score lower on college admissions tests, thus many capable youth are denied entrance or access to so-called "merit" scholarships, contributing to the huge racial gap in college enrollments and completion.

High-stakes testing also causes additional damage to some students who are categorized as English language learners (ELLs). The tests are often inaccurate for ELLs, according to FairTest, leading to misplacement or retention. ELLs are, alongside students with disabilities, those least likely to pass graduation tests.

African Americans, especially men, are disproportionately placed or misplaced in special education, frequently based on test results. In effect, the use of high-stakes testing perpetuates racial inequality through the emotional and psychological power of the tests over the test takers.

And although most test makers screen test items for obvious bias, their efforts often do not detect *underlying* bias in the test's form or content.

Bias in Education

As you read, consider the following questions:

1. How does Tyner refute the idea that standardized tests by themselves lead to inequities in assessing applicants for college?
2. Why does Tyner believe that standardized tests are not preventing minority students from attending college?
3. According to the viewpoint, what have recent studies revealed about supposed bias toward certain college applicants?

Recent years have seen many colleges and universities adopt "test-optional" admissions, but the evidence to date suggests that such policies will have, at most, small effects on the equity objectives that are often rhetorically tied to those policies. Other elements of the application packet exhibit gaps that are similar to those observed in exam scores, and evaluations of test-optional admissions policies show little effect on equity.

Policy Implications

1. Institutions should not decide whether to rely on college admissions exams based on concerns that they are racist or otherwise bad for equity.
2. More generally, because the best predictions of students' program success will come from analyses that include a variety of measures, institutions should require and examine a range of relevant and predictive data for admissions. The key criterion for inclusion of a measure ought to be its value for predicting program success rather than its correlation with student background factors.
3. States should require and pay for all high school students to take the SAT or ACT, in order to help identify all students with high academic potential, especially those from underrepresented groups.

The following brief evaluates the extent to which the use of college entrance exam scores by higher education institutions contributes to differences in college admissions and completion observed across racial/ethnic and socioeconomic groups. It evaluates five statements that have become the conventional wisdom among parts of the public or policymaking community, including the following: "College admissions exams are racist," "College admissions exams limit students' pathways into quality higher education," "Other parts of college application packets promote equity better than entrance exams," "Admissions officers should just focus on grades," and "The future of college admissions is 'test optional.'"

"College admissions exams are racist." No.

In a landmark 2021 settlement by the University of California (UC), the nation's most prestigious state university system, officials agreed to eliminate the requirement that students submit college entrance exam scores to gain admission. When then-UC president Janet Napolitano initially proposed suspending the testing requirement in 2020, her statement argued that eliminating testing requirements would "enhance equity," a claim that has become increasingly prevalent among opponents of college entrance exams in particular and standardized testing in general. In education, "inequity" typically refers to gaps in the outcomes experienced by different groups of students, but critics of college admissions exams have often gone even further, painting the SAT and ACT as simply racist. For example, the left-leaning groups that brought the UC lawsuit called the tests "discriminatory," and their lawsuit cited then-UC regent Cecilia Estolano, who said of the SAT, "We all know it's a racist test." From lawsuits to deliberate test-blind or test-optional admissions policies, the claim that the SAT and ACT put underrepresented minority students at a disadvantage is pervasive.

Gaps in average exam scores for students of different groups are, of course, no myth. The average ACT composite score is about

Bias in Education

20, but the highest-scoring racial/ethnic group, Asian students, scores 24.9 on average, while Black students, the lowest-scoring group, have an average score of 16.3. For some, the existence of such a gap is alone sufficient to prove the tests are racist. Yet students of different groups do not all have the same family and school experiences. Black children, for example, are three times as likely as their Asian and white classmates to grow up in poverty. Childhood disparities in access to everything from health care to good schools and teachers mean that—whatever those disparities say about the roots and consequences of American inequality—it would be surprising if all groups of 17-year-olds exhibited equivalent levels of college readiness. As we will see below, all measures of academic achievement exhibit such gaps.

Far from being instruments of systemic racism, the SAT and ACT are put through extensive measures to ensure that the exams do not discriminate against students because of their racial or ethnic background (or class or gender). The organizations that administer the exams vet them intensely, not just by diverse review panels that alert the test makers to any potential cultural biases but also through statistical techniques that flag test questions answered differently by students from different backgrounds. This latter process alerts test makers to any questions that, after controlling for students' overall scores, two groups of students (e.g., students from high-income and low-income families) answer correctly at different rates. Officials at both testing companies implement multiple, overlapping systems designed to ensure that the exams are free of such biased questions before they could affect any student's score.

"College admissions exams limit students' pathways into quality higher education."
Yes, but only for a few students.

For admissions exams to harm equity in higher education, students would have to lose access to college because of their exam scores. In fact, only a minority of students attend colleges where a high exam score is required for admission in the first place. Regardless of race or social class, most students attend institutions where either no score is required at all or only a very low score is needed to gain admission.

The admissions testing landscape has changed dramatically since the COVID-19 pandemic, and as of writing, few colleges require testing. Yet even before COVID-19, it was rare for students to need good ACT or SAT scores to access higher education. More than one in three undergraduates in the U.S. attends "open-access" two-year institutions (i.e., community colleges), which require neither exam scores nor a good grade point average (GPA), and many four-year institutions do not require test scores either. Many less-selective four-year institutions are either open-access or very nearly so in practice, and a number of prestigious four-year institutions offer access through high school GPA or class rank (e.g., the University of Texas), completing community college with an adequate GPA (e.g., the UC system), or through long-standing test-optional policies (e.g., the University of Chicago).

This does not mean that admissions exam policies are irrelevant. Of course, some students will seek to attend highly selective colleges where good test scores are essential. Others will need to take the exams to qualify for scholarships or to enroll in selective programs within a less-selective institution, such as honors colleges or rigorous majors such as engineering. Yet even though exam scores are important to some students, students have long had access to most American institutions of higher education without ever taking a college entrance exam.

"Other parts of the college application promote equity better than entrance exams." **Not necessarily.**
Most prospective students who attend colleges that are at least somewhat selective submit application packets that include such materials as the following:

- College admissions exam scores
- Personal essays

- Letters of recommendation
- Information about extracurricular activities
- Credit-by-examination scores (e.g., Advanced Placement [AP])
- High school transcripts, which themselves include the following:
- Name and location of the high school attended
- Courses taken
- Grades

Critics of college entrance exams implicitly suggest that the other application components do not exhibit the same gaps. Otherwise, there is nothing special about the exam scores, so it is not clear why excluding them would make admissions more equitable.

But are gaps among students unique to entrance exams? In fact, what research exists on other elements of the application packet strongly suggests they are responsible for "perpetuating inequities" in much the same way.

Consider a 2020 study that used software to analyze hundreds of thousands of student admissions essays from applications to the University of California system. The study, which was the first to use quantitative methods to analyze college admissions essays, found that the form and content of students' personal essays were even more correlated with student socioeconomic status than SAT scores. (The researchers did not examine differences in essays by racial/ethnic group.)

Letters of recommendation exhibit gaps as well, although their magnitude appears smaller. A 2018 study identified disparities by race and gender for undergraduate letters of recommendation, although that study characterized the gaps as "small but statistically significant." A 2020 study of recommendation letters for a graduate program also found differences depending on student background factors, including that the letters disproportionately described Black and Latino applicants as having "less agency" than other students. Such differences have led commentators to condemn the practice of requiring letters of recommendation in audacious terms, such as when a 2021 op-ed by a professor at the University of North Carolina deemed the letters "tools of oppression."

Gaps in participation in extracurricular activities are also apparent. A 2018 study found that extracurricular participation in high school is strongly linked to race and even more strongly correlated with family income. The gap between more- and less-affluent students is about 15 percentage points (40 percent versus 55 percent). More troublingly, the recent "varsity blues" scandal provided a particularly corrupt example of how selective schools can use policies favoring students who participate in extracurricular activities to admit students from wealthy and well-connected families; given the lack of transparency, "holistic" admission policies open the door to many such types of corruption.

The other data evaluated by admissions officers, from AP test scores to high school grades, all exhibit such gaps. Regarding AP, schools serving disproportionately low-income, rural, Black, and Hispanic students are less likely to offer advanced high school coursework such as AP and dual-enrollment courses. And even when students have access to these courses, the AP test scores themselves exhibit gaps. Although GPA is often touted as a better metric than test scores—as we will see below—it is correlated with race and socioeconomic status of students, as well.

The magnitudes of the gaps across measures vary, and in some cases, as with admissions essays, they are probably even larger than those for test scores. Still, these disparities are difficult to compare because of differing methodologies across studies. A 2019 report by the Georgetown University Center on Education and the Workforce found that the students selected solely based on the SAT would, on average, hail from wealthier families and be more likely to be white and Asian than under the status quo. That might seem like damning evidence against college admissions exams, but because the status quo includes affirmative action policies, it remains unclear whether the SAT (or ACT) gaps are actually greater than those for other admissions application components.

The fact that we observe similar kinds of gaps between student groups on every observable educational outcome suggests that these data simply reflect society's broader inequities. Thus, patterns in SAT and ACT scores offer a window into a society that has not done enough to make up for its sordid racial history or continuing inequities, but blaming the exams for having gaps is a classic case of "shooting the messenger." College entrance exams are no more "tools of oppression" than letters of recommendation or anything else in the application packet. Indeed, any meritocratic admissions process that uses academic data is likely to exhibit similar gaps.

"Admissions officers should just focus on grades." Wrong.

Grades and GPA are often identified by equity advocates as a good alternative to test scores, as they tend to be less correlated with socioeconomic status and race/ethnicity. Yet, like other components of the college application packet, analyses reliably show that grades are still correlated with student background factors, including race and family income. At most, replacing test scores with grades might mitigate the racial or socioeconomic disparities within higher education admissions, but the disparities would not be eliminated.

Interestingly, a 2007 study by researchers from UC Santa Barbara shows how grading standards vary across schools and finds that, within a given high school, grades correlate with socioeconomic status to a similar extent as test scores. This underscores another advantage of college admissions exams over grades: they're a more objective yardstick. Grades and high school course taking (as well as other elements of the application packet) are valuable data points for admissions officers to consider, but many are difficult to compare across schools. Exam scores can reveal school quality, which is why admissions officials—even those from "test-blind" or "test-optional" institutions—often use such data to help them rate the high schools of prospective students and to contextualize GPA.

This is why studies predicting postsecondary success have consistently shown that admissions exam scores provide additional information over and above what GPA can show. Yet grade inflation is squeezing high school GPAs into an ever-narrower range, suggesting they will eventually be less valuable to admissions officers as markers of achievement and, thus, predictors of college readiness. Although an earlier analysis showed that GPA was still a useful predictor of readiness 15 years ago, studies since then have found continued high school grade inflation (amid other evidence of softening high school standards). Still, even if GPA continues to be a better predictor of college success than exam scores, the best predictions are typically derived from analyses that include a variety of relevant measures. This means that institutions should require and examine a range of relevant and predictive data for admissions. The key criterion for inclusion of a measure ought to be its value for predicting program success rather than its correlation with student background factors.

"The future of college admissions is 'test-optional.'" Unclear.

For some colleges, SAT and ACT scores may be expendable, and going test optional or test blind will not harm their selection processes. Yet it is clear that some institutions find the information these exams provide to be valuable. One example is MIT, which reinstated pre-pandemic testing requirements in 2022. Their dean of admissions explained that "considering performance on the SAT/ACT, particularly the math section, substantially improves the predictive validity of our decisions with respect to subsequent student success at the Institute." Moreover, he argued that considering admissions exam scores was good for equity as well, as "not having SATs/ACT scores to consider tends to raise socioeconomic barriers to demonstrating readiness for our education." Other faculty and administrator groups, including the UC Faculty Senate task force (which was ultimately ignored) and a group of 60 law school deans in an open letter from 2022, have challenged the trend toward ignoring admissions tests. Because higher education stakeholders face different challenges, we shouldn't be surprised that admissions exams will not be used in a uniform manner in all American colleges.

In fact, admissions officers have myriad data available to assess student readiness, even as GPA becomes a less-reliable measure and admissions exam scores have increasingly become optional. With all the other data available, standardized admissions exams may provide only marginal additional information for individual students. Such tests provide an objective measure of academic preparation, but they are one tool among many, and their results should not be thought of as the one indispensable indicator of college readiness. Still, because many institutions are likely to use these scores in the foreseeable future, and because excellent students at mediocre schools might otherwise be overlooked, there is an obvious implication for state policymakers: states should require and pay for all high school students to take the SAT or ACT, in order to help identify all students with high academic potential. Over the years, such state policies have proven themselves to be a boon to equity.

Considering that the tests are closely vetted to remove biased content, irrelevant to many admissions decisions, and correlated with student background in a similar way to other elements of the college application packet, it shouldn't be a surprise that when institutions go "test optional," it is not the radical step toward equity that many assume. A 2015 study found that liberal arts colleges that implemented test-optional admissions policies did not become substantially more diverse. Instead, the main effect of the policies was to render greater "perceived selectivity" for such institutions. In effect, switching to test-optional policies, rather than being a win for social justice, may be more a kind of virtue signaling by these elite institutions.

More institutions may choose to engage in this kind of virtue signaling, and test-optional policies may endure or spread. Or perhaps high school grade inflation will lessen the value of high school GPA, and more institutions will require entrance exam scores to validate student preparation. Or maybe both trends will occur for different types of institutions. Regardless, institutions should not decide whether to rely on college admissions exams based on concerns that they are racist or otherwise bad for equity. Whether the exams are required or not, the implications for equity are minimal.

VIEWPOINT 3

> *"The wealth gap between white and Black families remains as wide as it was in 1968, hurting the ability of Black families to pay for test-prep courses and private college counseling services."*

The College Admissions Process Is Racist
Elizabeth Redden

In this viewpoint, Elizabeth Redden writes about the inherent racism in college admissions practices. Minority students are far less likely to gain admission to prestigious colleges than their white counterparts. Part of this, she admits, is monetary. Colleges value upper-middle-class and wealthy students who can pay tuition, preferring them for admission over those who cannot pay full college prices or who need scholarship money to attend. Many colleges have done well to eliminate or minimize the effects of standardized test scores on admissions, but in doing so they need to be more transparent about what other criteria are being used. Colleges need to match their rhetoric concerning diversity with actual admissions practices, Redden writes. Elizabeth Redden is a senior reporter for Inside Higher Ed *who covers general higher education topics, religion and higher education, and international higher education.*

"Confronting Racism in Admissions," by Elizabeth Redden, Inside Higher Ed, October 25, 2020. Reprinted by permission.

Are School and College Admissions Processes Unfairly Biased?

As you read, consider the following questions:

1. How are legacy admissions a detriment to a diverse student population, according to the viewpoint?
2. What are the problems with eliminating standardized testing?
3. What developments have occurred in the battle over affirmative action?

The barriers to admitting more Black students to the nation's selective universities are numerous and well-known.

Research shows college admission officers focus recruiting efforts on wealthy, predominantly white high schools.

Black students are far more likely to attend high-poverty schools and to have less access to core college preparatory classes in math and science.

Black students earn lower scores, on average, on standardized college admission tests such as the SAT and ACT.

The wealth gap between white and Black families remains as wide as it was in 1968, hurting the ability of Black families to pay for test-prep courses and private college counseling services. And Black students leave college with higher amounts of student debt than white students, impacting both their college experiences and their future prospects.

Legacy admission preferences favor wealthy white students, perpetuating long-standing inequalities in college access.

And in some states, prohibitions on affirmative action preclude any consideration of race in the admissions process.

A recent report by the Education Trust on Black and Latinx enrollment at 101 selective public colleges found only 9 percent enroll Black students at rates proportionate to their population within the state. The organization, which advocates for educational opportunities for all students with a focus on students of color, found that the percentage of Black students at nearly 60 percent of the institutions has actually fallen since 2000.

The report makes a number of recommendations, including increasing access to "high-quality" high school guidance counselors and using race more prominently in admission decisions. The report also advocates rescinding state bans on affirmative action, increasing aid to Black and Latinx students, adjusting recruitment strategies, improving campus racial climates, changing funding incentives, and reducing the role of standardized testing in admissions or going test optional.

"There is no acceptable reason in 2020 for the vast majority of these 101 public colleges to systematically exclude Black students like this—and to a great extent, Latino students as well," said Andrew Howard Nichols, the author of the report and senior director for research and data analytics at the Education Trust. "It is past time for public college presidents to take substantive antiracist action that matches their soaring antiracist rhetoric."

Many college leaders issued statements speaking out against racism and affirming their institutions' commitments to diversity and inclusion in the wake of the killings by police of George Floyd and Breonna Taylor. But moving those stated commitments from mere words to actual action in the midst of the pandemic will be undoubtedly be challenging, especially at a time when colleges are under more financial pressure than ever before—and under more critical scrutiny for their handling of both racial issues and their response to the public health emergency.

"A lot of institutions are going to be thinking, we need more students who can pay tuition by going for upper-middle-class students, for example, who are predominantly white. That's all well and good if you're thinking from a tuition standpoint, but not from an equity standpoint," said W. Carson Byrd, a sociologist and scholar in residence at the University of Michigan's National Center for Institutional Diversity. "As more institutions find themselves in more difficult financial times, how much are they going to turn away from their statements about racial equity and instead go back to … the economic factors that are important? For me it's a both/and; it's not an either/or."

From Conversation to Action

Marie Bigham, a former college admissions professional and the executive director of ACCEPT, a group that advocates for racial equity in college admissions, said people in the field talk a lot about racial equity.

"We've been stuck in conversation as opposed to pushing toward action, but now we're in a space where everything's pushing us toward action," she said. "The racial reckoning happening in higher ed is forcing action."

"One of the easy immediate fixes that colleges can put into place at this moment to get beyond statements of equity is get rid of legacy admissions right now, across the board, and get rid of demonstrated interest as an indicator in the process at all," Bigham said.

Demonstrated interest refers to admissions offices tracking ways in which students interact with them, by visiting campus or engaging on social media, for example. Colleges use demonstrated interest as a measure because they think an engaged applicant is more likely to accept an admission offer.

Longer term, Bigham said, "I think we as admission professionals, we've got to become vocal about financial aid, reforming that system from top to bottom."

ACCEPT co-organized a research initiative, Hack the Gates, which culminated over the summer with the publication of a series of policy papers focused on equity in college admissions.

A paper by Ted Thornhill, a sociologist and associate professor at Florida Gulf Coast University, advocates for systematically auditing admission officers' email correspondences with students to ensure they are equally responsive to prospective students and applicants across different socio-demographic groups. Thornhill's past research has shown that fictional Black students who emphasize Black identity or racial activism in email messages to admissions officers are less likely to receive responses than Black students who send messages lacking explicit mention of race.

He argued admissions professionals "should be advocating at their own institutions in a really serious way to bring about greater racial equity. What kinds of institutions are you bringing students into?" he asked.

"You sing the praises, the institutional line, about all the positive things you do and how you help students cultivate a body of knowledge and a skill set that will serve them well in their future endeavors. You say all that, but most of these predominantly white institutions are deeply racist."

The Standardized Testing Piece

One area in admissions where there has been rapid change since the start of the pandemic is in the movement to make standardized tests optional.

The number of institutions going test optional was already growing fast but accelerated after the pandemic forced the cancellation of test administrations. FairTest: National Center for Fair and Open Testing, a group that advocates for test-optional policies, reported in September that 1,570 four-year colleges across the U.S. will not require applicants to submit a SAT or ACT score for fall 2021 admission. Test-blind or test-optional institutions now account for more than two-thirds of all four-year institutions in the U.S., according to FairTest's count.

Researchers have found mixed results as to whether test-optional policies lead to increases in enrollment of low-income and underrepresented minority groups. Testing companies have argued that using standardized test scores alongside other measures, including grades, provides a more accurate and complete view of student performance compared with using any one measure alone.

Even those who advocate for test-optional policies argue they are not a "silver bullet." Dominique J. Baker, assistant professor of education policy at Southern Methodist University, and Kelly Rosinger, an assistant professor of education at Pennsylvania State University, noted in a recent article published in *Education Next* that "test scores are not the only source of bias in the selective admissions process."

"Race and class inequalities are baked into many of the metrics that selective colleges use to evaluate applicants," Baker and Rosinger wrote. "For instance, there are decades of research demonstrating that low-income students and students of color have less access to the advanced high-school coursework that selective colleges view as a measure of a rigorous curriculum. While selective colleges try to evaluate applicants in the context of their individual high schools and communities—that is, taking into account whether students took advantage of the most difficult coursework available to them—other common metrics used to evaluate students may also reflect racial and class privilege."

The topic of test-optional admissions — and what colleges rely on if they *don't* use a standardized test score — came up at a recent town hall meeting on systemic racism and college admissions organized by the National Association for College Admission Counseling in June.

"Every time someone says 'test optional,' I feel like somebody should say 'transparency,'" said Tevera Stith, one of the panelists and vice president for KIPP Through College & Career for the KIPP public schools in Washington, D.C. "There are schools who have long done test optional … but they're not transparent about how those applications are reviewed, so first I would put the onus on my colleagues at the college level in college admissions offices to be transparent about how they're making those decisions."

Ericka Matthews-Jackson, senior director of undergraduate admissions at Wayne State University in Detroit and another panelist at the NACAC town hall, said the pandemic "pulled the scab off the wound really quickly" in terms of colleges' reliance on test scores.

"Now a lot of institutions are going to have to grapple with how do we change with our admissions policies and what things are going to be important to us rather than us taking the easy route and saying, 'Oh yeah, you have this test score and this GPA; therefore you get admitted,'" Matthews-Jackson said at the event.

"I think it's going to require more than just taking a look at essays. There's a lot of things to take a look at when you're considering what a student has gone through to get to the point where they're ready for college, what kind of high school were they educated in, what kind of resources did they have available, what did they avail themselves of in terms of educational opportunities prior to them coming. Are they first generation to go to college; is English their second language? There are so many things that we should be considering and looking at, because we do want to have institutions that represent our communities."

Systemic Bias in Private Schools Reinforces Societal Inequality

In today's society, systemic bias continues to be a pervasive issue that hinders marginalized individuals from accessing private school opportunities. This not only perpetuates inequality but also exacerbates the lack of fairness, equity, and inclusion in our education system.

Private schools are often seen as a gateway to success, offering enhanced resources, smaller class sizes, and a more personalized approach to education. However, the reality is that these opportunities are not equally accessible to all. Systemic bias, rooted in socioeconomic disparities, race, and other factors, creates barriers that prevent marginalized individuals from benefiting from private school education.

One of the key ways systemic bias affects marginalized communities is through financial constraints. Private schools often come with hefty tuition fees, making them unaffordable for many low-income families. This perpetuates a cycle of disadvantage, as those who cannot afford private school education miss out on the advantages it offers, further widening the achievement gap.

Moreover, systemic bias also manifests in the admissions process of private schools. Unconscious biases can influence decision-making, favoring applicants from privileged backgrounds and perpetuating

Considering Race

What about considerations of race?

Fewer than 7 percent of colleges—6.8—say race or ethnicity has "considerable influence" on admission decisions, while 17.8 percent say it has "moderate influence" and 16.9 percent "limited influence," according to NACAC's 2019 "State of College Admission" report.

Well over half—58.4 percent—said race or ethnicity has no influence on their admission decisions.

The use of race in college admission decisions is, of course, an exceedingly controversial and legally contested topic, subject of multiple Supreme Court cases stretching back to 1974. The

---

the exclusion of marginalized individuals. This not only limits their access to quality education but also reinforces societal inequalities.

The consequences of this systemic bias are far-reaching. Marginalized individuals are denied the opportunity to develop their full potential, hindering their social mobility and perpetuating generational poverty. Furthermore, the lack of diversity within private schools hampers the development of inclusive and empathetic communities, hindering the growth of a fair and equitable society.

To address this issue, it is crucial to implement policies that promote fairness, equity, and inclusion in private school admissions. This includes providing scholarships and financial aid to ensure that students from all socioeconomic backgrounds can access private education. Additionally, schools must actively work to eliminate unconscious biases in their admissions processes, ensuring equal opportunities for all applicants.

In conclusion, systemic bias in private school opportunities is a pressing issue that perpetuates inequality and hampers fairness, equity, and inclusion. By acknowledging and addressing these challenges, we can work towards a more just and inclusive education system that empowers all individuals, regardless of their background, to thrive and succeed.

"Systemic Bias and Private School Opportunities: Navigating Challenges," Honor Society Foundation, October 29, 2022.

Supreme Court has upheld the consideration of race in admissions, most recently in the second Fisher v. Texas case in 2016.

However, legal challenges contesting the scope of the use of race in admission persist and have kept colleges on the defensive.

Harvard University successfully defended itself in a federal lawsuit last year alleging its admission policies discriminate against Asian Americans. The case is now being heard in a federal appeals court.

Earlier this month, the U.S. Department of Justice sued Yale University over its admission policies and accused it of illegal discrimination against Asian American and white applicants. Yale's president, Peter Salovey, described the lawsuit as "baseless" and defended the university's admission practices as "completely fair and lawful."

Meanwhile, nine states—California, Florida, and Michigan being among the biggest and Idaho being most recent—have adopted bans on race-based affirmative action. Public universities in a 10th state, Georgia, dropped the use of race in admissions after losing a court challenge in 2000.

A study of the effect of these state-level bans published earlier this year in the journal *Educational Evaluation and Policy Analysis* found "the elimination of affirmative action has led to persistent declines in the share of underrepresented minorities among students admitted to and enrolling in public flagship universities in these states."

Policy change may be coming, at least in California. The Board of Regents for the University of California unanimously voted in June to endorse the repeal of the state's nearly quarter-century-old prohibition on using race- and gender-based preferences in admission decisions at public universities. California residents will vote on whether to repeal the affirmative action ban in November.

The UC system maintains that "despite years of effort with race-neutral admissions," its enrollment of students from underrepresented minority groups—and its recruitment of faculty of color—"falls short of reflecting the diversity of California's population."

Among the steps UC has taken over the years is the introduction of a program in 2001 called Eligibility in the Local Context, which guarantees admission to students graduating in the top 9 percent of each participating high school, and the development of a holistic review process for undergraduate admission in which students are "evaluated for admission using multiple measures of achievement and promise while considering the context in which each student has demonstrated academic accomplishment."

"We think that in a university as large and as complex as ours, that uses as many as 14 different characteristics to evaluate candidates for admission, that we can implement a 15th characteristic to help us find the right cross-section of students," said John A. Pérez, chair of the regents.

"It's not just about race," he said. "It's also about gender. We can't use either, and would argue that the evidence is pretty clear. There is no proxy for gender; there is no proxy for race. You could find a bunch of workarounds or you can be honest and forthright. What we're saying is we should be able to have an honest, forthright evaluation of the totality of factors that make someone who they are and speak to that which they've achieved."

Among the opponents to ending the affirmative action ban in California is former UC regent chair, Ward Connerly, who led the campaign for the 1996 ballot measure Proposition 209, which imposed the ban in the first place. He is chairman of Californians for Equal Rights, the campaign to reject the repeal of Proposition 209. The campaign has been endorsed by a coalition of community organizations, including a number of groups representing Asian Americans, who fear they will be disadvantaged in admissions by the introduction of race-based preferences.

Connerly argued Prop 209 didn't ban affirmative action, per se.

"It bans discrimination and preferential treatment and it's those last two words that create heartburn for the practitioners of affirmative action, because they know in their heart of hearts as they practice it, it really does amount to different standards for different groups on the basis of race and color," he said. "They can justify that, but I can't, because I'd have to believe that Black people and Latinos are inherently unable to compete alongside whites and Asians for admission to the University of California, and I don't believe that. It's not an accurate premise. It's racist in its own self."

VIEWPOINT 4

> "If [colleges] wanted to create classes that were more socioeconomically balanced, they could already do so from their current applicant pool. They choose not to because their goal is, in part, to run the nation's elite families through their institutions in order to increase their endowments and power in society."

Ivy League Admissions Purposely Favor the Rich

Matt Bruenig

While many who argue for a more egalitarian college admissions system want to eliminate standardized test scores, Matthew Bruenig says that doing so actually has the opposite effect. Wealthy students often do even better than their less affluent peers when they are judged by grades, recommendations, and extracurriculars. Bruenig argues that if selective colleges really wanted to create a fairer system, they would. But they don't want to, he suggests, because maintaining a haven for society's elite is a quiet part of their mission. Wealthier students and their families contribute dollars to a school's endowment, and a large endowment is a measure of a school's prestige. Matthew Bruenig is an American lawyer, blogger, policy analyst, commentator, and founder of the left-leaning think tank People's Policy Project.

"Ivy League Admissions Favor the Rich by Design," by Matt Bruenig, Jacobin, July 25, 2023. Reprinted by permission.

Bias in Education

As you read, consider the following questions:

1. According to Bruenig, what are some methods that selective colleges can use to eliminate their bias toward the rich?
2. What does Bruenig mean when he says that seats at prestigious colleges are being misallocated?
3. According to Bruenig, how should elite universities attempt to fix the system?

Egalitarian reformers have argued that elite college admissions should focus less on test scores and more on personal statements, extracurriculars, and recommendation letters. New research suggests that this approach only further favors the wealthy.

Raj Chetty, David Deming, and John Friedman put out a study this week that, among other things, tries to identify whether rich people are disproportionately admitted to top universities and, if so, why. This has been a topic of intense interest in the discourse for as long as I have been involved in it, and I think this study helpfully resolves some of the long-standing disputes in that discourse.

For starters, while it is true that children from the richest families have better academic qualifications than the population overall, it is not true that this fully explains their greater representation in the top universities. After controlling for test scores, the richest kids are admitted at more than twice the rate as the population overall. Notably, this admissions boost is found among the 12 Ivy-Plus schools analyzed in the study, but not at flagship public universities.

Despite what some think, the overrepresentation of the rich at the top universities is not driven solely or even primarily by legacy preferences. According to the paper, after controlling for test scores, legacy preferences explain about 30 percent of the surplus rich attendees, while higher application rates, higher matriculation rates, better nonacademic credentials, and athlete preferences explain the remaining 70 percent.

If you take application rates and matriculation rates out of the equation, leaving only the factors related to how universities make admissions decisions, legacy preferences account for 46 percent of the surplus rich attendees, while better nonacademic credentials account for 30 percent, and athlete preferences account for the remaining 24 percent.

A debate has raged for many years about how much weight to put on test scores versus grades and nonacademic factors. One popular view that has emerged on the Left is that test scores should be augmented, if not entirely replaced, by more holistic considerations like personal statements, extracurricular activities, recommendations, and things of that nature. This view appears to be primarily motivated by the belief that such augmentation will benefit kids from poorer families.

The alternative view is that these holistic considerations actually favor the rich more, because the rich will tend to accumulate better recommendations, more extracurricular activities, and even better grades because they have more information and are more strategic about preparing a college resume.

This study suggests that the alternative view is the correct one. When comparing students with similar test scores, every other consideration—including academic ratings (grades), nonacademic ratings (extracurriculars), guidance counselor recommendations, and teacher recommendations—favors the rich, with extracurriculars and recommendations especially favoring the rich.

If the goal is to eliminate the extent to which rich kids are overrepresented at top universities relative to their test scores, the study points to the existence of some fairly straightforward ways to do so. Legacy and athlete preferences can be zapped immediately. Nonacademic factors like recommendations and extracurriculars could be hugely down-weighted or eliminated entirely. Other targeted encouragement could increase the application and matriculation rates of the nonrich.

But this is really not the goal of top universities. These schools already have vastly more qualified applicants than they have seats. If they wanted to create classes that were more socioeconomically balanced, they could already do so from their current applicant pool. They choose not to because their goal is, in part, to run the nation's elite families through their institutions in order to increase their endowments and power in society.

Insofar as a hugely outsize share of the ruling class of the country matriculates through these institutions, it makes sense that they are objects of intense scrutiny. Anything that has to do with the creation and reproduction of the ruling class should be of interest to the public, because it has an impact on everyone.

However, many people seem to be interested in these institutions because they think that they are important pieces of our higher education system when that just is not the case. According to the study, the 12 Ivy-Plus schools have an average admissions class of 1,650 and admit around 157 more rich kids than they ought to based on test scores alone. This means that, between these schools, there are around 1,884 seats being misallocated to the rich every year. By comparison, around 4 million kids are admitted at undergraduate institutions in a given year.

The kids who are elbowed out by the 1,884 nondeserving rich kids still attend college, just at a 98th percentile institution, not a 99th percentile institution. The quality of the educational services they receive does not differ, though the prestige, status, and career opportunities made available by their institution does.

Egalitarian reforms to the higher education system should focus on reducing selectivity and making top universities less distinct from the rest of the system. Swapping a few thousand people around the top few percentiles of the university system just isn't going to do much to create an equal or fair society, if it does anything at all.

VIEWPOINT 5

> "Partisans largely differ in their opinions on how colleges and universities considering race and ethnicity in admissions decisions affects students, the college environment, and equal opportunity in the country."

Americans Are Divided About Issues of Race and College Admissions

Pew Research Center

In this viewpoint, the Pew Research Center reports the results of its 2023 survey on factoring race into college admissions. Beliefs about the legitimacy of doing so hinge largely on whether those asked were liberal or conservative. The latter group was far more likely to consider affirmative action unfair. But beliefs around race and college admissions also vary depending on one's ethnicity and education level, among other factors. What really stands out in the survey is that Americans are very divided when it comes to questions about race and college admissions. The Pew Research Center is a nonpartisan fact tank that informs the public about the issues, attitudes and trends shaping the world. They conduct public opinion polling, demographic research, content analysis, and other data-driven social science research.

"Perceived impacts of factoring race and ethnicity into college admissions," Pew Research Center, June 8, 2023.

opportunity for Americans of all racial and ethnic backgrounds than they are to say this is bad (47 percent vs. 29 percent).

However, Asian adults also are more likely to say considering race and ethnicity makes the overall admissions process of these colleges less fair than to say it makes it more fair (53 percent vs. 18 percent).

Asian adults are also more likely to say the students accepted to schools that take race and ethnicity into account in admissions decisions are less qualified (36 percent) rather than more qualified (17 percent). About a third (34 percent) say accepted students are neither more nor less qualified.

Hispanic adults, on balance, view factoring race and ethnicity into college admissions as having a positive impact on ensuring equal opportunity for Americans of all racial and ethnic backgrounds (47 percent say it is good, while 23 percent say it is bad).

But Hispanic adults are more divided over the effect on the fairness of the admissions process (36 percent say it makes the process less fair, 28 percent say it makes the process more fair) and the impact it has on the qualifications of admitted students (19 percent say it results in less-qualified students, while an identical share say it results in more-qualified students).

Educational Differences

Those with bachelor's degrees or more formal education are generally more likely to offer an opinion on what the effects are of considering race and ethnicity in college admissions decisions, and their responses are generally more positive.

For instance, college graduates are more likely than those without a degree to say that the consideration of race and ethnicity has positive effects on students' educational experiences (39 percent vs. 21 percent, respectively) or ensuring equal opportunity for all Americans (47 percent vs. 31 percent).

However, in their assessments of the fairness of these processes, similar shares of those with a college degree or more education (53 percent) and those with some college experience or less education (47 percent) say considering race and ethnicity as a factor in admissions decisions makes the overall admissions process less fair.

Supporters and Opponents of Considering Race and Ethnicity in College Admissions Highlight Different Areas of Impact

Those who approve and disapprove of considering race and ethnicity in college admissions have starkly different evaluations of the effects of these practices. Opponents are particularly likely to see this practice as making admissions less fair, while supporters are particularly likely to see it as having a positive effect on ensuring equal opportunity for all Americans.

Those who disapprove of the consideration of race and ethnicity in admissions decisions overwhelmingly (78 percent) say this makes the overall admissions process less fair. Views about the effect on the fairness of admissions are more mixed among those who approve of taking race and ethnicity into account: By more than two-to-one, more say this makes the process more fair (46 percent) than less fair (20 percent), while about three-in-10 (29 percent) say it does not affect the overall fairness of admissions.

A narrow majority of disapprovers (55 percent) say that the students accepted by schools that consider race and ethnicity in admissions are less qualified than if the schools did not consider this as a factor. Just 6 percent say they are more qualified, while about a quarter (27 percent) say there is no difference in qualifications. In contrast, a majority—60 percent—of those who approve of taking race and ethnicity into account in selective college admissions say that accepted students under these practices are neither more nor less qualified, while 21 percent say they are more qualified and 12 percent say they are less qualified.

Roughly six-in-10 of those who approve of the consideration of racial and ethnic background in admissions (61 percent) say that students' overall educational experience is better at colleges that do this, while 7 percent say the educational experience is worse. Among disapprovers, 44 percent say this makes educational experiences worse, while 10 percent say this makes it better. About a third of those who disapprove of these practices (34 percent) and about a quarter of those who approve (27 percent) say it has neither effect.

Approvers and disapprovers are far apart in their views of whether the consideration of race and ethnicity in selective college admissions contributes to equal opportunity for Americans of all racial and ethnic backgrounds. Around three-quarters of approvers (73 percent) say these practices are good for ensuring equal opportunity, compared with 16 percent of disapprovers. A majority of disapprovers (55 percent) say it is bad for ensuring equal opportunity when colleges take race and ethnicity into account (just 7 percent of approvers say this).

About Four-in-Ten Adults See Negatives, No Positives from Race and Ethnicity Factoring into College Admissions; 30 Percent See Only Positives

Roughly four-in-10 adults (41 percent) express negative views and have no positive views of the outcomes that result when colleges consider race and ethnicity in college admissions—meaning they offer at least one negative assessment and no positive assessments across all four survey items about different effects of admissions practices that consider race and ethnicity.

Three-in-10 adults express some positive views and no negative views, while 15 percent express a mix of both positive and negative and 14 percent express exclusively neutral assessments (including "neither" and "not sure" response options) on all four items.

Roughly half of white Americans (49 percent) offer only negative and neutral views, a far higher share than among Americans of other racial and ethnic backgrounds.

Black Americans are more likely than those in other groups to offer no negative views (46 percent of Black adults provide only positive and neutral responses to all four questions).

Asian Americans are more likely than those in other groups to express a mix of positive and negative assessments of the impact of these practices: 26 percent of Asian adults have a mix of positive and negative views, compared with 18 percent of Hispanic adults and 13 percent each of white and Black adults.

A majority of Republicans (65 percent) express no positive views on the four items, though there are substantial differences between white and Hispanic Republicans. Seven-in-10 white Republicans express no positive views, compared with 48 percent of Hispanic Republicans. And a quarter of Hispanic Republicans express no negative views, compared with just 8 percent of white Republicans.

About half of Democrats (49 percent) express no negative views of colleges considering race and ethnicity in admissions, with only modest differences between racial and ethnic groups among Democrats.

Personal Experiences with Efforts to Increase Racial and Ethnic Diversity

When asked whether they have ever personally been at a disadvantage in their education, career, or job because of efforts to increase racial and ethnic diversity, Americans are about twice as likely to say they have *not* ever been at a disadvantage as to say they have (57 percent vs. 24 percent).

Republicans are 8 percentage points more likely than Democrats to say they have ever personally been at a *disadvantage* (28 percent vs. 20 percent). Within racial and ethnic groups, 35 percent of Black, 27 percent of Asian, 23 percent of white, and 20 percent of Hispanic adults report ever having been at a disadvantage.

About one-in-10 adults (11 percent) say they have ever personally been at an *advantage* in their education or career due to efforts to increase racial and ethnic diversity. Similar shares of Black (20 percent), Asian (18 percent), and Hispanic adults (15 percent) say this, compared with 7 of white adults.

Black adults are more likely than those of other racial and ethnic backgrounds to say that other people have assumed they benefited unfairly from efforts to increase racial and ethnic diversity: 28 percent of Black adults say this has happened to them, 6 points higher than the share of Hispanic adults who say this. Smaller shares of Asian (13 percent) and white adults (10 percent) say this has happened to them.

Periodical and Internet Sources Bibliography

The following articles have been selected to supplement the diverse views presented in this chapter.

Jeremy Bauer-Wolf, "Rich students are twice as likely to get into prestigious private institutions than lower-income peers with similar test scores, a new study says," *Higher Ed Dive*, July 24, 2023. https://www.highereddive.com/news/here-are-3-admissions-practices-that-favor-wealthy-students-at-top-ranked-c/688775/.

Aatish Bhatia, Clair Cain Miller, and Josh Katz, "Study of Elite College Admissions Suggests Being Very Rich Is Its Own Qualification," the *New York Times*, July 24, 2023. https://www.nytimes.com/interactive/2023/07/24/upshot/ivy-league-elite-college-admissions.html.

Jessica Bryant, "Most Young People Think College Admissions Decisions Are Biased, Report Finds," August 21, 2023, *Best Colleges*. https://www.bestcolleges.com/news/analysis/young-people-think-college-admissions-are-biased.

Emma Camp, "Is This the End of the Ivy League Nepo Baby?," *Reason*, July 5, 2023. https://reason.com/2023/07/05/is-this-the-end-of-the-ivy-league-nepo-baby/.

Daniel de Visé and Lexi Lonas, "Are legacy admissions on the way out?," the *Hill*, September 4, 2023. https://thehill.com/homenews/education/4183749-are-legacy-admissions-on-the-way-out/.

Sarah Hinger, "Moving Beyond the Supreme Court's Affirmative Action Rulings," ACLU, July 12, 2023. https://www.aclu.org/news/racial-justice/moving-beyond-the-supreme-courts-affirmative-action-rulings.

Scott Jaschik, "Wealth and Admissions," *Inside Higher Ed*, March 17, 2019. https://www.insidehighered.com/admissions/article/2019/03/18/look-many-legal-ways-wealthy-applicants-have-edge-admissions.

Neil Lewis, Jr., "Are Standardized Tests Racist, or Are They Anti-Racist? Yes," the *Atlantic*, January 23, 2023. https://www.

theatlantic.com/science/archive/2023/01/should-college-admissions-use-standardized-test-scores/672816/.

Katharine Meyer and Adrianna Pita, "How will the Supreme Court's affirmative action ruling affect college admissions?," Brookings, June 30, 2023. https://www.brookings.edu/articles/how-will-the-supreme-courts-affirmative-action-ruling-affect-college-admissions/.

Monica Potts, "Most Americans Wanted The Supreme Court To End Affirmative Action — Kind Of," *538.com*, June 29, 2023. https://fivethirtyeight.com/features/american-opinion-affirmative-action/.

Lisa Shambaugh, "Developing a Bias-Aware Admission Process," National Association of Independent Schools, Fall 2018. https://www.nais.org/magazine/independent-school/fall-2018/developing-a-bias-aware-admission-process/.

Zachary B. Wolf, "Race neutral' replaces affirmative action. What's next?," CNN, July 1, 2023. https://www.cnn.com/2023/07/01/politics/affirmative-action- race-neutral-what-matters/index.html.

OPPOSING VIEWPOINTS® SERIES

Chapter 3

Is the Current Political Divide Harming Education?

Chapter Preface

"When you put political officials in charge of education, you get politicized education," writes J. D. Tuccille in the magazine *Reason*. Nowhere has this been more apparent than in the battle over the New College of Florida in Sarasota.

The New College was founded in 1960 and had built an enviable reputation as a prestigious institution for serious students. However, in 2023, Florida Governor Ron DeSantis, acting on information that the New College was a bastion of liberalism, orchestrated a hostile takeover. The New College, mind you, was not any more liberal than many other Florida universities. Most college campuses are fairly liberal. The New College had only earned three of five stars on the Campus Pride Index, which rates how LGBTQ+ friendly a campus is. By comparison, Ithaca College, in a famously liberal small city in upstate New York, received five stars.

But the New College of Florida was still too liberal for DeSantis' tastes. In a campaign carried out in early 2023, the governor overhauled the college's board of trustees, appointing six new members, including Christopher Rufo, Matthew Spalding, Charles R. Kesler, Mark Bauerlein, Debra Jenks, and Eddie Speir. The first four are conservative activists who do not live in Florida. At its first meeting on January 31, 2023, the new board summarily fired President Patricia Okker "without cause" and installed Richard Corcoran, a political supporter of the governor, as its new president. While Okker was making about $200,000 a year, Corcoran's salary for the same position reputedly is in excess of $1 million.

Additional changes to the college followed: the university's diversity and equity office was dissolved; bans were implemented on using personal pronouns in email signatures by faculty; and events promoting diversity and inclusion were canceled. Board member Christopher Rufo announced that the college would be shutting down "ideologically captured academic departments and hiring new faculty" such as the Department of Gender Studies. Another goal was to drive liberal students from the university and replace them with young scholars more to their liking. As a result, the New College's entry test scores have dropped sharply.

Students were not the only ones driven from the university. As of early 2024, approximately 40 percent of the school's faculty resigned or went on leave. As Herb Guggenheim writes, "The school is now guilty of the kind of politicization DeSantis accused liberals of practicing—a forced externally imposed ideology."

If the New College was an isolated instance, the situation would not be so dire. After all, most colleges in the U.S. lean left, and so there should be room for conservative establishments, though not perhaps at the expense of teachers and students who previously enjoyed their academic lives at the New College of Florida.

But the New College is not an isolated instance. All over the country, conservative activists have decided that taking over educational institutions is important for their political future. Supporters argue that this is a necessary course-correction for an already politicized field, while detractors assert that this practice is negatively impacting the education of students across the country.

The effort to bring more conservative voices into education has not been limited to post-secondary education. All over the U.S. conservatives have been trying to take over school boards and establish "parental rights." Consequently, debates over whether education has a liberal or conservative bias are more timely than ever before.

VIEWPOINT 1

> *"There is an undercurrent of dissatisfaction—even suspicion—among the public about the role colleges play in society, the way admissions decisions are made, and the extent to which free speech is constrained on college campuses. And these views are increasingly linked to partisanship."*

Americans' Opinions About Higher Education Are More Divided than Ever

Pew Research Center

In this viewpoint, the Pew Research Center reports on its findings from a 2019 study regarding the partisan divide in how Americans view higher education. While a majority of Americans recognize the value of a college education, many are becoming suspicious or dissatisfied with what they believe is occurring on campuses. An ever-increasing number of conservatives feel that many colleges have a liberal bias. Liberals, on the other hand, are concerned more with the ever-rising cost of college tuition, room and board, and fees. The partisan gaps that underlie these views are reflective of our politics more broadly, the authors suggest. The Pew Research Center is a nonpartisan fact tank that informs the public about the issues, attitudes, and trends shaping the world. They conduct public opinion

"The Growing Partisan Divide in Views of Higher Education," Pew Research Center, August 19, 2019.

polling, demographic research, content analysis, and other data-driven social science research.

As you read, consider the following questions:

1. How has confidence in the value of a college degree changed in recent years?
2. How do those polled feel about whether college curricula are politically biased?
3. How does conservative opinion on the purpose of college differ from liberal opinion?

Americans see value in higher education—whether they graduated from college or not. Most say a college degree is important, if not essential, in helping a young person succeed in the world, and college graduates themselves say their degree helped them grow and develop the skills they needed for the workplace. While fewer than half of today's young adults are enrolled in a two-year or four-year college, the share has risen steadily over the past several decades. And the economic advantages college graduates have over those without a degree are clear and growing.

Even so, there is an undercurrent of dissatisfaction—even suspicion—among the public about the role colleges play in society, the way admissions decisions are made, and the extent to which free speech is constrained on college campuses. And these views are increasingly linked to partisanship.

A new Pew Research Center survey finds that only half of American adults think colleges and universities are having a positive effect on the way things are going in the country these days. About four-in-ten (38 percent) say they are having a negative impact—up from 26 percent in 2012.

The share of Americans saying colleges and universities have a negative effect has increased by 12 percentage points since 2012. The increase in negative views has come almost entirely from Republicans and independents who lean Republican. From 2015 to 2019, the share saying colleges have a negative effect on the country went from 37 percent to 59 percent among this group. Over that same period, the views of Democrats and independents who lean Democratic have remained largely stable and overwhelmingly positive.

Gallup found a similar shift in views about higher education. Between 2015 and 2018, the share of Americans saying they had a great deal or quite a lot of confidence in higher education dropped from 57 percent to 48 percent, and the falloff was greater among Republicans (from 56 percent to 39 percent) than among Democrats (68 percent to 62 percent).[1]

Two additional Pew Research Center surveys underscore the partisan gap in views about higher education. In late 2018, 84 percent of Democrats and independents who lean to the Democratic Party said they have a great deal or a fair amount of confidence in college and university professors to act in the best interests of the public. Only about half (48 percent) of Republicans and Republican leaners said the same. In fact, 19 percent of Republicans said they have no confidence at all in college professors to act in the public interest. And in early 2019, 87 percent of Democrats—but fewer than half (44 percent) of Republicans—said colleges and universities are open to a wide range of opinions and viewpoints.

Republicans and Democrats Differ Over What's Ailing Higher Education

A 2018 Pew Research Center survey took a deeper dive into the reasons for these shifting views. The survey first asked whether the higher education system in the U.S. is generally going in the right or wrong direction. A majority of Americans (61 percent) say it's going in the wrong direction. Republicans and Republican leaners are significantly more likely to express this view than Democrats and Democratic leaners (73 percent vs. 52 percent).

Among those who say higher education is headed in the wrong direction, some of the reasons why they think this is the case differ along party lines. Majorities of Republicans (77 percent) and Democrats (92 percent) say high tuition costs are a major reason why they believe colleges and universities are headed in the wrong direction.

Democrats who see problems with the higher education system cite rising costs more often than other factors as a major reason for their concern, while Republicans are just as likely to point to other issues as reasons for their discontent. Roughly eight-in-10 Republicans (79 percent) say professors bringing their political and social views into the classroom is a major reason why the higher education system is headed in the wrong direction (only 17 percent of Democrats say the same). And three-quarters of Republicans (vs. 31 percent of Democrats) point to too much concern about protecting students from views they might find offensive as a major reason for their views. In addition, Republicans are more likely than Democrats to say students not getting the skills they need to succeed in the workplace is a major reason why the higher education system is headed in the wrong direction (73 percent vs. 56 percent).

There are significant age gaps among Republicans in these views. Older Republicans are much more likely than their younger counterparts to point to ideological factors, such as professors bringing their views into the classroom and too much concern about political correctness on campus. For example, 96 percent of Republicans ages 65 and older who think higher education is headed in the wrong direction say professors bringing their views into the classroom is a major reason for this. Only 58 percent of Republicans ages 18 to 34 share that view.

A 2017 Gallup survey found similar partisan divides when it asked those who expressed only some or very little confidence in U.S. colleges and universities why they felt that way. Democrats tended to focus more on costs and quality, with 36 percent volunteering that college is too expensive, 14 percent saying colleges have poor leadership and are not well run, and 11 percent saying the overall quality of higher education is going down. Republicans focused more on political and ideological factors: 32 percent said colleges and universities are too political or too liberal (only 1 percent of Democrats volunteered this type of response). And 21 percent of Republicans pointed to colleges not allowing students to think for themselves and pushing their own agenda as reasons why they didn't have a lot of confidence in them.

Another national survey conducted last year by Boston-based WGBH News looked more closely at views about the political climate at colleges and universities. A majority of adults (59 percent) said politics on college campuses lean toward a particular viewpoint, while 28 percent said campuses are nonpartisan. Of those who thought politics lean toward one particular viewpoint, 77 percent said they lean liberal, while 15 percent said they lean conservative. About half (47 percent) of those who see an ideological tilt at colleges and universities said this is a major problem, while 32 percent said it's a minor problem.

These views differed substantially by party. A majority of Democrats (60 percent) said students are hearing a full range of viewpoints on college campuses, but only 26 percent of Republicans shared that view.[2] In addition, Republicans were much more likely than Democrats to see a political leaning on college campuses: 72 percent of Republicans compared with 48 percent of Democrats said campuses lean toward one particular viewpoint. Among those who saw a political leaning, majorities of Republicans (85 percent) and Democrats (68 percent) said campuses lean more liberal than conservative. But Republicans were much more likely than Democrats to say that campuses leaning toward a particular viewpoint is a major problem—67 percent of Republicans vs. 26 percent Democrats said this.

Views on the College Admissions Process

The equity of the college admissions process has come into question recently, with many concerned that wealth and privilege are having an undue influence. Earlier this year, the College Board announced that it will begin including an "adversity score" along

The Scarcity of Conservative Faculty in Higher Education

The overwhelming majority of faculty on campuses nationwide have long fallen on the left of the political center. In a 2018 article for the right-leaning nonprofit advocacy group National Association of Scholars, economist Mitchell Langbert concluded that, excluding the two military colleges, the ratio of registered Democrats to Republicans among faculty at liberal arts colleges is 12.7 to 1.

Lewis said the political leanings of faculty generally matter more in the social sciences, while his sense is that in the hard sciences the politics of faculty members are less likely to play a role in their work.

"In the hard sciences, I generally have no idea what my colleagues' politics are since it has zero impact on their scholarship," he said. "If you're in economics, or in political science, or in sociology, probably people's political views are closer to the surface."

Government professor Ryan D. Enos disagreed with Lewis, asserting that politics can infuse into all disciplines, even if it appears apolitical at the time.

"We may look around now and say people are just doing science, which of course a lot of people in the social sciences say they are too, but it may not be evident to us at the time that what we're doing is highly politicized," Enos said.

Enos added that Harvard faculty across all disciplines would be more likely to have "pretty intense" political views than the average American, since political involvement is highly correlated with education.

In an emailed statement, former University President Lawrence H. Summers wrote that he believes academia is naturally more "progressive" because professors are choosing to forego more lucrative job opportunities.

"People who don't like capitalism tend to gravitate to academia because they don't like working for companies, whereas people who like capitalism have many more choices," Summers wrote.

"'An Endangered Species': The Scarcity of Harvard's Conservative Faculty," by Natalie L. Kahn, the Harvard Crimson, April 9, 2021.

with a student's SAT score in an effort to provide more information about students' educational and socioeconomic backgrounds.

According to the WGBH News survey, the vast majority of Americans say it's important for colleges and universities to have a diverse student body in terms of race and ethnicity. About six-in-10 (63 percent) say this is extremely or very important and an additional 22 percent say it's somewhat important. Only 13 percent say diversity on campuses is not important.

However, a recent Pew Research Center survey finds that the public is not in favor of colleges and universities considering race or ethnicity in making admissions decisions. Some 73 percent of all adults say race or ethnicity should not be a factor in college admissions decisions. About one-in-five (19 percent) say this should be a minor factor and 7 percent say it should be a major factor. Majorities across racial and ethnic groups—62 percent of Blacks, 65 percent of Hispanics, 58 percent of Asians, and 78 percent of whites—say race and ethnicity should not be a factor in admissions decisions. Republicans are more likely than Democrats to say race and ethnicity shouldn't be a factor in admissions decisions, but majorities of both groups express this view (85 percent among Republicans, 63 percent among Democrats).

So what factors does the public think should drive admissions decisions? High school grades top the list—67 percent say grades should be a major factor in making these decisions, and 26 percent say they should be a minor factor. About half (47 percent) say standardized test scores should be a major factor, and 41 percent say they should be a minor factor.

Those two largely objective factors stand out among other potential admissions criteria. Fewer adults say community service involvement (21 percent cite this as a major factor, 48 percent minor) or being a first-generation college student (20 percent major, 27 percent minor) should be factors in making college admissions decisions. And fewer still say that athletic ability (8 percent major, 34 percent minor) or legacy status (8 percent major, 24 percent minor) should be factors.

In some cases, college graduates have different views on this than those who did not graduate from college. For example, while 57 percent of those with a four-year college degree say whether someone is the first in their family to attend college should be a major or minor factor in making admissions decisions, 43 percent of those without a bachelor's degree say the same.

The Value of a College Degree

Despite the public's increasingly negative views about higher education and its role in society, most Americans say a college education is important—if not essential—in helping a young person succeed in the world today. A 2018 Center survey found that 31 percent of adults say a college education is essential, and an additional 60 percent say it is important but not essential. However, far higher shares say a good work ethic (89 percent), the ability to get along with people (85 percent), and work skills learned on the job (75 percent) are essential for a young person to succeed.

When it comes to their own experiences with higher education, an earlier Center survey found that the vast majority of college graduates (from both two- and four-year institutions) say college was useful for them in terms of helping them grow personally and intellectually (62 percent say it was very useful in this regard, 31 percent say it was somewhat useful). Large majorities also say it was useful in opening doors to job opportunities (53 percent say very useful, 29 percent say somewhat) and in helping them develop specific skills and knowledge that could be used in the workplace (49 percent very, 35 percent somewhat).

Still, the public remains skeptical that today's colleges are preparing people for the workforce. Only 16 percent say a four-year degree from a college or university prepares someone very well for a well-paying job in today's economy, while 51 percent say it prepares them somewhat well. Community colleges get even less positive marks: 12 percent say a two-year degree from these colleges prepares someone very well for a job, and 46 percent say it prepares them somewhat well.

These views generally don't differ markedly by educational attainment. Among adults with a four-year college degree or higher, 13 percent say a four-year degree prepares someone very well for a well-paying job; 11 percent of those with an associate degree say the same, as do 12 percent of those with some college experience but no degree and 17 percent of those with no education beyond high school. However, among those who didn't complete high school, a much higher share—40 percent—say a four-year college degree prepares someone very well for a well-paying job.

Republicans and Democrats have similar opinions on this, although Democrats are more likely than Republicans to say a four-year degree prepares people somewhat well for a high-paying job in today's economy.

There's a larger party gap in views on the main purpose of college. A majority of Republicans (58 percent) say it should be to teach specific skills and knowledge that can be used in the workplace, while only 28 percent say it should be to help an individual grow personally and intellectually. Democrats are more evenly divided on this: 43 percent say the main purpose of college should be developing skills and knowledge, while roughly the same share (42 percent) point to personal and intellectual growth.

Even amid doubts about the extent to which college prepares people for today's job market and disagreement about what the role of college should be, the fact remains that a four-year college degree has very real economic benefits. The income gap between college graduates and those without a bachelor's degree has grown significantly over the past several decades. In 1990, the median annual earnings for a full-time worker ages 25 to 37 with a bachelor's degree or higher was $53,600. At the time, this compared with $40,200 for a worker with some college experience but no bachelor's degree and $33,600 for a worker with no college experience. In 2018, the difference was even more pronounced: $56,000 for a worker with a bachelor's degree or more education, $36,000 for someone with some college education, and $31,300 for a high school graduate.

This broad overview of data on views about higher education in the U.S. reveals a complex set off attitudes—a public that still sees the benefit of a college education but has grown wary about the politics and culture on college campuses and the value of a four-year degree that has an ever-increasing price tag.

The partisan gaps underlying these views are reflective of our politics more broadly. From health care to the environment to immigration and foreign policy, Republicans and Democrats increasingly see the issues of the day through different lenses. But views on the nation's educational institutions have not traditionally been politicized. Higher education faces a host of challenges in the future—controlling costs amid increased fiscal pressures, ensuring that graduates are prepared for the jobs of the future, adapting to changing technology and responding to the country's changing demographics. Ideological battles waged over the climate and culture on college campuses may make addressing these broader issues more difficult.

VIEWPOINT 2

> "Thus, as a result of brain drain and self-sorting, Americans are now more likely to live in communities where they are isolated from people who hold different ideologies and values."

Brain Drain Is Deepening the Political Divide
Rachel Sheffield and Scott Winship

Rachel Sheffield and Scott Winship point out that educated Americans are more and more gravitating away from rural communities and relocating to urban centers, most of which are located on the West and East Coasts. While educated people are more likely to move in general, brain drain is continuing to increase. This relocation of highly educated people causes economic and political issues for the communities they're leaving. With the educated moving out of certain states, their economies take a hit. Furthermore, as Republicans tend to live in more rural areas and Democrats in more urban enclaves, the political divide only deepens. It is easier to blame the other side when you don't interact with any of them, the authors suggest, but the political divide harms everyone. Scott Winship is a senior fellow and the director of the Center on Opportunity and Social Mobility at the American Enterprise Institute. Rachel Sheffield is a Research Fellow in welfare and family policy at the Heritage Foundation.

"Brain Drain and the Polarization of America", by Rachel Sheffield and Scott Winship, The American Conservative, May 3, 2019. Reprinted by permission.

As you read, consider the following questions:

1. What is "brain drain," according to the viewpoint?
2. In what specific ways does brain drain hurt the economy?
3. What are the negative effects of social segregation?

Are we more divided as a nation today than we were before? Our new research within the Joint Economic Committee's Social Capital Project suggests that we are. The findings indicate that Americans are more frequently dividing themselves geographically and along lines of education. Highly educated Americans have increasingly moved to a handful of states over the last several decades, leaving other places behind.

This "brain drain" has clear economic implications. Beyond economics though, it's also likely draining social capital from many places, as communities lose talent and resources that would help support civic institutions. Brain drain and educational sorting exacerbate political and cultural divides as well: Americans segregate themselves into communities where they more frequently reside near those similar to themselves, decreasing the likelihood of rubbing shoulders with those who see the world differently.

The Rust Belt, the Plains, and some states in New England are experiencing high levels of brain drain.

It's not news that highly educated Americans are more likely to move. America's highly educated have consistently been more prone to pack up their bags and seek opportunity outside their hometowns. But surprisingly, there have been few attempts to quantify the magnitude of the problem and assess whether it is getting worse. To rectify that, we created brain drain measures that compare the share of people leaving their birth states who are highly educated to either the highly educated share of people staying in their birth states or the share entering the states who are highly educated. We found that today, highly educated movers in the U.S. tend to leave certain states and regions of the country at higher rates than in the past and concentrate in a smaller group of states that are home to booming metropolitan areas. This leads to growing geographic divides between areas that are thriving and places that struggle. With fewer states retaining and attracting talent, more areas are left behind.

A handful of states have become exclusive destinations for the highly educated. They not only hold onto more of their homegrown talent, but they also gain more highly educated adults than they lose. These talent-magnet states are along the West Coast, as well as the Boston-Washington corridor.

Beyond the coasts, a few other states, like Texas, are retaining their homegrown talent while simultaneously winning a balance of talent from elsewhere.

These "brain gain" states are like an elite club whose members trade among themselves. For example, California draws the greatest share of its highly educated entrants from other brain gain states: New York, Illinois, and Texas, which are ranked third, fourth, and eighth, respectively, on net brain gain. New York pulls in highly educated entrants primarily from New Jersey (ranked sixth on net brain gain) and California. Massachusetts (ranked second) is also among its top five sending states. The most common origins of Texas's entrants include California, Illinois, and New York. New Jersey draws its highly educated from the likes of New York, Massachusetts, California, and Illinois. New York and New Jersey are among Massachusetts' most common sending states. New York, New Jersey, California, and Virginia (ranked seventh) are among the top states sending highly educated natives to Maryland.

On the opposite side of the coin are the many states that are not only bleeding highly educated adults but failing to attract others to replace them. Rust Belt states—Pennsylvania, Ohio, Indiana, Michigan, Wisconsin, and Missouri—are particularly plagued by brain drain. Several Plains states—Iowa and the Dakotas—as well as states in New England—Vermont and New Hampshire—are also experiencing high levels of brain drain. Although this is hardly a new phenomenon for the Rust Belt, it's become a worsening problem over the last 50 years for the other high brain-drain states mentioned.

Brain drain's effects on state economies are obvious. Places that lose more of their highly educated adults are likely going to be economically worse off than those that retain or attract highly educated adults. And if the highly educated are concentrating in fewer areas, then more parts of the country will be prone to economic stagnation. But beyond the economic implications, brain drain also has an impact on social capital. If areas are drained of their most highly educated, those left behind may struggle to support churches, athletic leagues, parent-teacher associations, scouting groups, and so forth. These institutions matter for the well-being of communities, as they bring people together in purposeful relationships, ultimately creating the social fabric of our nation.

Another way that brain drain's educational divides can deplete social capital is by creating deeper political and cultural divides between Americans. The highly educated more often hold liberal political views compared to those with less than a college education. America's major metropolitan areas (many of the states that win the highly educated are home to thriving cities) tend to vote Democratic, while most other areas of the country vote Republican. Those living in urban areas are also more likely to hold liberal political views, whereas those living in rural areas are more commonly conservative.

Thus, as a result of brain drain and self-sorting, Americans are now more likely to live in communities where they are isolated from people who hold different ideologies and values. Less association between people of different viewpoints can exacerbate political divides, as people become more steeped in their own beliefs. When those who are different are further away, it is easier to cast them as a faceless group of opponents upon whom all blame for America's problems belongs, rather than as neighbors with whom to find common ground. Ultimately, social segregation weakens the idea that, as Americans, we share something important in common with one another.

A growing federal government only adds to the problem of geographic divide. Naturally, neither heartland traditionalists nor coastal cosmopolitans want to be ruled by the other camp. However, with more power at the national level, national elections have higher stakes for everyone. Each camp feels threatened when its party loses control. With less association among those with different viewpoints, political discourse turns into fever-pitched discord.

The strength of our relationships is crucial to the strength of our nation. Americans will have to work to make their communities places in which not only the most highly educated benefit, but others as well. We must find ways to reach across the divides that separate us.

VIEWPOINT 3

> "The vast majority of red states are rural and more homogenous in population with conservative values focused on limited government and low taxes; blue states, and the Democratic Party, are characterised by the concentration of their population in more liberal and diverse urban centers and increasingly liberal suburban areas."

Red and Blue States Battle Over Higher Education Policy

John Aubrey Douglass

In this viewpoint, John Aubrey Douglass surveys the state of higher education in a politically divided United States. Douglass covers a variety of higher education issues, including loan forgiveness, educational bias, the effect of the red state–blue state battle on higher education, and more. He looks into how states like Florida are replacing higher education heads with political allies and disrupting the usual state of instruction, and he looks at how future elections may affect the state of higher education. In summary, he notes that elections matter, and that colleges and universities will remain subject to the wishes of politicians. John Aubrey Douglass is a senior research fellow and research professor in public policy

"Blue versus red states: Higher education policy-making in the US," by John Aubrey Douglass, University World News, January 21, 2023. Reprinted by permission.

and higher education at the Center for Studies in Higher Education (CSHE) at the University of California, Berkeley.

As you read, consider the following questions:

1. According to the author, why were President Joe Biden's plans to forgive student debt impractical?
2. How does the author characterize red states versus blue states?
3. What are some specific examples cited in this viewpoint of politicians affecting teaching in higher education?

The midterm elections in the United States brought a sort of victory for President Joe Biden and the Democrats, including the retention of a slim majority in the Senate and ceding only a marginal majority to Republicans in the House of Representatives.

Avoided was an expected much bigger electoral victory by Republicans and a clear majority in both houses of Congress. The net result for federal higher education policy is relative stability, although with some important caveats, including debates on raising the debt level of the federal government.

A reminder that in the US there is no ministry of education. Federal policy is largely limited to financial aid in the form of grants and loans to individual students and funding by multiple agencies for academic research. There is a lesser but important role involving the approval of independent accrediting agencies and monitoring for violations of civil rights by the U.S. Department of Education.

Most funding and regulatory power lies with state governments and their elected lawmakers. Hence, many of the battles and debates over higher education are at the state level, and here we see a significant difference in the political environment between 'blue' (Democratic majority) and 'red' (Republican majority) states.

Debates at the Federal Level

This does not mean that national political leaders do not use their position, rhetoric, and sometimes vitriol to blame universities and colleges for an array of ills—including high tuition fees and alarming student debt levels incurred more significantly at private and for-profit institutions (with mostly affordable publics lost in the national discourse).

Donald Trump and many in his party have also painted academic communities as oppressive liberal bastions intolerant of conservative viewpoints and champions of wokism—not all entirely incorrect and powerfully echoed in conservative media outlets.

Through it all, and as noted, Biden's higher education agenda remains relatively intact as we move into 2023.

This includes a successful marginal increase in the Pell Grant—the primary federal loan program for lower-income students. Under his administration, the federal government also allocated substantial COVID relief funds to help universities temporarily transition to more online courses and to cope with losses in tuition revenue due to falling enrolments in many states.

Biden made campaign promises to make community colleges free—a vast network of primarily two-year colleges offering vocational and adult programs and courses that can lead to transferring to a four-year institution. He also planned to cancel student debt for a large portion of former students, whether they graduated or not.

But those two unrealistic promises have morphed over the last year or so. The free community college bid was in part Biden's effort during the 2020 democratic presidential primary to provide a version of proposals by competitors, like Bernie Sanders, for free public university and college, with no regard to a student's individual or family income.

As in other parts of the world, free higher education is popular, even if it is largely an incomplete thought when it comes to how to pay for it.

The proposal for free community colleges (virtually all of which are public, local based and largely funded institutions) fell with the failure of a previously U.S. $3 trillion and expansive "Build Back Better" proposal by Biden and liberal democrats.

Later, Biden, using his powers as an adept moderate and compromiser and with slim majorities in the House and Senate, got a smaller funding package passed that focused on rebuilding America's eroding infrastructure. The free community college scheme was dropped. The earlier campaign proposal lacked specificity as to how it would work and its potential progressive impact.

Existing fees are very low in these local institutions and most low-income students already have access to Pell Grants and other forms of financial aid that make study tuition free or nearly so for the most needy; the bigger problem is that many students do not know about the various federal and state financial aid programs and how to apply for aid.

No-tuition-fee schemes at non-selective higher education institutions also correlate with high drop-out rates and an inefficient use of taxpayer dollars.

Student Debt

Similarly, Biden offered a more moderate proposal for relieving, if not ending, student debt than many of his Democratic rivals in the presidential election.

Instead of a blanket debt relief promise for all, no matter their income, he and his policy advisors imagined a more narrow program for those who took out federal loans: debt relief of up to U.S. $10,000 per former student and an additional U.S. $10,000 for those who had a Pell Grant but also took on additional federal loans.

About half of all past students in the U.S. took out a student loan. Of those who did, 32.2 percent owe U.S. $10,000 or less in federal debt, and 74.2 percent owe U.S. $40,000 or less—not counting those who took out debt at the postgraduate level to become lawyers, doctors, and other generally high-income professions.

The Biden plan is also income-dependent, offering debt relief for federal loans (not for private bank loans) to individuals making less than U.S. $125,000, or up to U.S. $250,000 for those jointly filing their tax return with their spouse or legal partner.

In the midst of the COVID pandemic, Biden had also previously suspended all federal loan repayments—part of the larger effort to mitigate the feared economic impact of the pandemic.

Biden's debt relief scheme applies to those who attended a tertiary education institution before 2020. Some 40 million Americans would be eligible at a cost of approximately U.S. $400 billion over 30 years. White House officials say the debt relief program is for lower- and middle-income families. How a couple making U.S. $250,000 is middle income is hard to fathom when the median household income in the U.S. is just over U.S. $70,000.

Most scholars and researchers who study financial aid have criticized the Biden plan as too generous and costly, and not targeted enough toward lower income former students. Conservatives also say the same, leading to a lawsuit that challenges the authority of the president to offer loan forgiveness on this scale without legislative approval.

It is important to note that a good portion of those who would be eligible for debt relief currently have sufficient earnings to pay their student debt. The federal spending would also ignore the many who have already diligently paid off their loans.

And then there is the inequality of providing this large tax-funded pay-out to those who willingly chose to enroll in a higher education institution and take on debt, a high percentage of whom never graduated. Those who did not go to college would be essentially subsidising those who did.

The legal challenge to Biden's debt relief program is now before the U.S. Supreme Court. While there is a need for debt relief, it appears the optics of providing blanket debt relief so desired by much of the Democratic base trumped a more strategic approach. The proposal also negatively plays into the narrative of many moderates and conservatives of a free-spending liberal Biden administration which lacks regard for the growing national debt.

While waiting for a decision by an extremely conservative Supreme Court that champions archaic notions of states' rights and that will likely overturn decades of precedent that allows universities to harness a measured approach to affirmative action, the Biden administration is also formulating an overhaul of the department's income-driven federal loan repayment program. In accordance with an announcement last week, undergraduate borrowers would have a cap in their repayment set at five percent of their discretionary income; graduate student borrowers' payments would be capped at 10 percent for their discretionary income.

The Story of Blue and Red States

In the most simple terms, there is a red and blue state divide when it comes to the role and importance of public institutions, including universities. There are also a handful of so-called purple states: states in which no one party has a significant majority of votes and which, for instance, might have a Democratic governor and a Republican majority in the state legislature.

While the Democrats picked up two additional governorships in the midterm elections, that did not substantially change the power dynamics between and among the states: the Republicans hold 28 out of 50 governorships and retain majorities in a similar number of state legislatures.

The vast majority of red states are rural and more homogenous in population with conservative values focused on limited government and low taxes; blue states, and the Democratic Party, are characterized by the concentration of their population in more liberal and diverse urban centers and increasingly liberal suburban areas.

Blue states tend to have higher educational attainment rates, including people with a bachelor degree. With some exceptions, they are also the hubs for technology and other growth economic sectors.

Most blue states, and their lawmakers, have a general sense of the value of public universities and colleges and are seeking paths to re-invest in them after the severe ebb of state funding before and during the Great Recession and the onset of the COVID pandemic.

In contrast, a Pew Research Center survey found that some 59 percent of Republicans feel that colleges and universities have a negative effect on American society, profess low esteem for professors, and feel that they are influenced by political leftist activism.

Red state politicians see an advantage in attacking universities as reinforcing the "deep state" and focusing on cultural issues revolving around race and gender fluidity debates.

To varying degrees, the Republican lawmakers have embraced many characteristics of right-wing neo-nationalism found in other parts of the world: meaning they are anti-immigrant, nativist, and isolationist, prone to anti-science rhetoric and policies, seek ways to gerrymander and control elections, and find subtle and sometimes overt ways to attack political opponents and gain greater control of public institutions, including universities and the judiciary.

At the same time, funding has generally improved for higher education in both red and blue states, in part because of the federal government's massive infusion of pandemic relief funding directed to state governments and a generally improving economy, despite high inflation rates.

Blue and red and purple, state politics also find consensus on the important role of tertiary institutions in workforce development and regional economic development.

Attacks on Higher Education

Governors in many red states have sought paths to populate public university governing boards and university presidencies with conservative loyalists.

In Florida, for example, Republican Governor Ron DeSantis, a presidential hopeful who now exceeds Trump in popularity among Republicans in recent polls, has repeatedly targeted universities, and schools in general, as proponents of critical race theory (CRT) and dogmatic enablers of LGBTQ rights.

In part based on a national legislative template offered by an activist conservative lobbying group, the Florida legislature passed a bill last May banning the teaching of CRT and restructuring tenure; another law allows students to record professors' lectures as evidence of possible bias.

Apparent fear of political and funding retribution led the president of the University of Florida, its flagship state university, to initially ban faculty from testifying against a DeSantis-backed effort to pass legislation widely believed to limit the voting rights of minority groups who more generally vote Democratic.

DeSantis also recently appointed a Republican senator from Nebraska, Ben Sasse, as president of the University of Florida despite significant protests from faculty. It is an odd fit.

Florida has become an important battleground regarding issues of academic freedom and university autonomy, but similar legislation has been passed or introduced in Oklahoma, Mississippi, North Dakota, Texas, and other states.

In Texas, the lieutenant governor voiced a common critique among conservatives regarding the flagship University of Texas campus in Austin, stating: "Tenured professors must not be able to hide behind the phrase 'academic freedom', and then proceed to poison the minds of our next generation…"

In Georgia, and despite widespread faculty protest, Republican Governor Brian Kemp appointed former two-term governor Sonny Perdue to lead the 26-institution University of

Georgia system; its governing board then made it easier to fire tenured professors.

Seeing into the Future

As we move into 2023, there are some signs of a more moderate political environment developing in the U.S., but also a probable gridlock in any meaningful policy-making at the federal level with the Republicans gaining their slim majority in the House of Representatives.

The ascending Republican leadership in the House remains fixated on retaining the old Trump political base and blocking any new initiatives from the Biden administration—whatever their merits.

Trump's errant higher education policies, including yearly proposed massive cuts in federal funding for academic research, were largely averted by a consensus of both parties in Congress.

The largest residue from the Trump period of chaotic policy-making is the rhetorical attacks on higher education and the broader effort to cast science and scientists as tools of a vast liberal conspiracy of disinformation.

With Trump's increased political and legal baggage, I think it unlikely for him, and his scorched earth policies, to return to the presidency. Without a clear agenda, or leader, and disarray in the Republican Party, much of Biden's agenda for higher education is in place and will shape the year ahead.

This includes the recent U.S. $1.7 trillion budget deal passed in late December and signed by Biden that includes a moderate but meaningful increase in funding to the National Science Foundation (NSF) and the National Institutes of Health (NIH).

Further bolstering federal funding for higher education, the recent CHIPS and Science Act will boost US microchip research and production and will funnel additional funding to academic researchers, helping to build generally positive collaborations between universities and the private high-tech sector that has fuelled economic growth.

These bipartisan deals also allowed the federal government to operate into early 2023. But there is uncertainty about the future of the federal budget that, in a worse case scenario, could mean cuts to mandated programs like Social Security and discretionary funding, like to the NSF and the NIH. Republicans have repeatedly used the arcane requirement for Congress to repeatedly increase the federal debt level, threatening to close down the government and growing political favor from the party's obstructionist base. As of this writing, they are doing this again, calling for more than $130 billion in unidentified cuts to the federal budget. Brinkmanship aside, one assumes that a deal will be made in the next five months or so and the U.S. will meet its debt obligations.

The economic fortunes of the U.S., and globally, will play a role in shaping domestic policy, along with the pending decisions by the Supreme Court on Biden's debt relief scheme and the probable decision to end America's brand of affirmative action at universities although the use of race and ethnic preferences in university and college admissions is in reality practiced by highly selective institutions that enrol only about 6 percent of all students.

As we move into the presidential race period, the red versus blue state dynamic, with political debates and news coverage often revolving around cultural issues that play well among Republican and many independent voters, will likely become even more heated. These are so-called "wedge" issues that drive tribal political actors and voters.

While much of this discussion is on domestic policy, there remains the important question of the path forward for the international engagement of higher education institutions in the U.S., including international research collaborations between universities and between scholars and students.

Russian President Vladimir Putin's savage attack on Ukraine and increasing tension with China regarding not only trade but science and technological espionage have created what might be termed a new and emerging academic cold war.

How the U.S., and the world, navigates this relatively new environment, and its influence on what has become an extremely robust global science system, is not clear.

On the one hand, it is leading to increased isolation for universities and academics in certain parts of the world, particularly Russia but also in an increasingly autocratic China. On the other hand, it may lead to an even more robust relationship with the European Union and possibly key portions of the Southern Hemisphere.

In the end, and as this short synopsis of contemporary higher education policy and politics in the U.S. shows, elections matter—at least in liberal democracies.

VIEWPOINT 4

> "Neutrality is itself a political choice, Dunn argues, and is one that bolsters the status quo. What results is a classroom that potentially ignores the fears, interests, and concerns of many students."

Education Is Inherently Political

Tim Walker

Tim Walker writes about how a teacher's decision to remain neutral on all topics—while seemingly desirable—can be detrimental to student learning. He warns that maintaining neutrality about controversial topics such as racism, inequality, and climate change is not a good policy. All education is politically and ideologically informed. This, according to Walker, became especially true with the presidency of Donald Trump. Many minority children, the viewpoint suggests, felt threatened by Trump's incendiary rhetoric. For a teacher to remain neutral when discussing his presidency may be harmful to such children, as it normalizes Trump's behavior. Parents and administrators may want teachers to shy away from political controversy, but, as Walker concludes, this is not always possible. Tim Walker is a senior writer for NEA Today.

"Education is Political': Neutrality in the Classroom Shortchanges Students," by Tim Walker, National Education Association, December 11, 2018. Reprinted by permission.

Bias in Education

As you read, consider the following questions:

1. According to Hadley Dunn, how is everything in education politically informed?
2. Why do many teachers fear speaking out about politics in the classroom?
3. According to the viewpoint, what methodology can help teachers to discuss politics in their classes?

When teaching about U.S. elections or politics, many educators will strive for neutrality. They may insist these discussions have no place in the classroom, while others argue that standardization and a lack of time make them a non-starter. Even if there was an opening, the slightest hint of bias could attract the ire of an administrator or parent. In this hyper-polarized political climate, that's a line that's easy to stumble across.

All this neutrality or avoidance may work for the teacher—but what about the student?

Alyssa Hadley Dunn, assistant professor of teacher education at Michigan State University, believes that a strict adherence to "neutrality"—not expressing your views to students and/or avoiding political topics—is a tactic that can actually marginalize many students.

Neutrality is itself a political choice, Dunn argues, and is one that bolsters the status quo. What results is a classroom that potentially ignores the fears, interests, and concerns of many students.

To be clear, Dunn is not talking about a teacher who stands in front of the class and reads aloud endorsements for local, state, and federal political office and then urges students to go home and tell their parents to vote accordingly.

The kind of neutrality that concerns Dunn is, for example, a decision to avoid discussion of "controversial" issues—racism, inequity, climate change, or gun violence, for example—out of fear of appearing political or partisan.

Education, at its core, *is* inherently political, says Dunn.

"Everything in education—from the textbooks to the curriculum to the policies that govern teachers' work and students' learning—is political and ideologically-informed," she explains. "Both what is taught and how it is taught is shaped by the cultural, social, political, and historical contexts in which a school is situated. We can't pretend that teachers can leave these contexts at the door."

Especially after the election of Donald Trump.

Although political polarization didn't begin with his candidacy, Trump's incendiary, crude, and divisive rhetoric about race, religion, gender, and immigration that marked his campaign (and his presidency) has been deeply unsettling to many, if not most, Americans.

According to a report by the Southern Poverty Law Center, the 2016 presidential campaign had a "profoundly negative effect on children and classrooms ... particularly acute in schools with high concentrations of minority children."

Yet, as Dunn and her colleagues Beth Sondel of the University of Pittsburgh and Hannah Carson Baggett of Auburn University concluded in a recent paper, many teachers continue to feel pressured to remain neutral when discussing Trump and are generally uncomfortable addressing racial and social justice issues in the classroom.

"This pressure (to stay neutral) is reflective of the lack of trust, autonomy, and professionalism for teachers in our current climate," the study, published in the *American Educational Research Journal*, concludes.

The researchers surveyed 730 teachers from 43 states to gauge how their pedagogical choices were affected after the election.

Some respondents made it very clear they did not adhere to what they saw as misdirected directives from school or district officials to stay away from anything Trump-related.

One middle school teacher explained that despite the fear many of his students had of deportation and harassment, "my school, tied by a never-ending desire to remain 'unbiased,' did nothing and told teachers to limit conversations about the elections because such conversations were not included [in the standards]."

"I don't care what my school administration says," the teacher continued. "My loyalty is to my students and their lives, . . . not to administrator requests to avoid conversations that are uncomfortable."

Generally, however, responses from educators were littered with words such as "fearful," "anxious," "unsure," and "scared," even as they acknowledged that a more engaged, proactive approach in the classroom may be necessary.

One educator from Massachusetts summed up the dilemma this way:

> "Trump unlike any other presidential candidate stands for everything I work to combat: racism, sexism, homophobia, and xenophobia. My students fall into categories of people he wants removed or controlled, in his America. I do not know how to talk to my students about this and be neutral (as per country policy)."

According to the study, teaching after the election was most challenging for those who were "ideological outsiders"—Clinton voters in areas where the majority of voters were pro-Trump and vice versa.

"Teachers had to negotiate if and how to talk about their own beliefs knowing that their students' parents and/or colleagues may disagree with them," Dunn says.

For example, an elementary teacher from a predominantly white school in Michigan explained,

> "I always feel nervous explicitly discussing politics in my classroom due to the variety of views of my students' parents and my own fear that parents will be upset or complain about me if my own views come up explicitly in classroom lessons/discussions. I know I have students whose parents supported both candidates passionately and I do sort of feel a responsibility to respect their parents' views (no matter how much I may disagree)."

It doesn't help that so much of our discourse is labelled "political" or "partisan," including discussions about human rights and social justice. Pedagogical choices, the researchers argue, should not be confined by this false construct.

"Making justice-oriented pedagogical choices is not about partisanship or controversy but, rather, is reflective of an overarching commitment to equity," they write.

Anchoring discussions to a justice and equity framework can provide educators with a path forward. Still, many of the respondents in the survey did not feel particularly well-prepared to take this on, let alone publicly challenge the presumed virtues of a neutral classroom. The study concludes that teacher training programs need to better prepare educators in adapting their classrooms to help students understand current events and political upheavals. The researchers recommend that current teachers, especially those "ideological outsiders," seek out networks across schools and districts that can serve as "restorative and supportive communities."

While Dunn and her colleagues are careful not to downplay the pressures educators face, they emphasize that, ultimately, teachers are charged with preparing their students to work toward a more democratic society.

With 2019 and 2020 shaping up to be just as tumultuous as the previous few years, what are the chances more educators will feel empowered and better prepared to talk politics (for lack of a better word) in their classrooms?

Don't count on the administration to lead the way, at least not yet. "Districts are still issuing bureaucratic demands on teachers that take their time away from the most important thing they can do in the classroom: create responsive and relevant curriculum for their students," explains Dunn.

And while too many parents still believe the classroom door should always be shut to any political discussion, they may be "ignoring the reality that such a move is never really possible," Dunn says.

Periodical and Internet Sources Bibliography

The following articles have been selected to supplement the diverse views presented in this chapter.

Johanna Alonso, "Chaos at New College of Florida," *Inside Higher Ed*, August 16, 2023. https://www.insidehighered.com/news/students/academics/2023/08/16/chaos-reigns-new-college-florida-fall-semester-nears.

Marilyn Anderson Rhames, "Are evangelical Christians abandoning public schools?," *Kappan*, August 23, 2021. https://kappanonline.org/are-evangelical-christians-abandoning-public-schools-pdk-poll-rhames/.

Joseph Contreras, "'Where learning goes to die': DeSantis's rightwing takeover of a liberal arts college," the *Guardian*, September 3, 2023. https://www.theguardian.com/us-news/2023/sep/03/new-college-florida-desantis-teachers.

Diana D'Amico Pawlewicz, "The Politics of Fear Is Damaging American Education—And Has Been for Decades," *Time*, December 14, 2023. https://time.com/6358167/school-politics-fear/.

Maureen Downey, "Is higher education biased against traditional Christians?" the *Atlanta Journal-Constitution*, July 16, 2017. https://www.ajc.com/blog/get-schooled/higher-education-biased-against-traditional-christians/OvUZDRhTjVTpPIb3oa9ALN/.

Alex Henderson, "The red state 'brain drain' is well underway — here's why," MSN, November 24, 2023. https://www.msn.com/en-ca/health/other/the-red-state-brain- drain-is-well-underway-here-s-why/ar-AA1ktorx.

Samantha Hernandez, "Investigating How Politics Is Affecting Education? Here's What to Know," Education Writers Association, September 13, 2022. https://ewa.org/news-explainers/how-politics-affects-education.

Brooke Migdon, "Nearly half of Republicans polled say schools shouldn't teach history of racism," the *Hill*, November 10, 2021. https://thehill.com/changing-america/enrichment/education/581029-nearly-half-of-republicans-polled-say-schools-shouldnt/.

Daniel Mollenkamp, "Teachers Feel the Strain of Politics. Can Better Political Engagement Help?" *EdSurge*, November 6, 2023. https://www.edsurge.com/news/2023-11-06-teachers-feel-the-strain-of-politics-can-better-political-engagement-help.

Billie Wright Dziech, "Higher Ed, We Have a Problem," *Inside Higher Ed*, September 20, 2023. https://www.insidehighered.com/opinion/views/2023/09/20/higher-ed-cant-afford-its-left-wing-bias-problem-opinion.

Megan Zahneis and Audrey Williams June, "In These Red States, Professors are Eyeing the Exits," the *Chronical of Higher Education,* September 7, 2023. https://www.chronicle.com/article/in-these-red-states-professors-are-eyeing-the-exits.

OPPOSING VIEWPOINTS® SERIES

CHAPTER 4

Is There Bias in Educational Curricula?

Chapter Preface

In March 2021, Republican activist Christopher Rufo spoke about critical race theory (CRT) in a lecture delivered at Hillsdale College:

> Critical race theory is fast becoming America's new institutional orthodoxy. Yet most Americans have never heard of it—and of those who have, many don't understand it. It's time for this to change. We need to know what it is so we can know how to fight it.

By November of the same year, a scant eight months later, Mark A. Thiessen wrote the following:

> By now, most Americans have heard of critical race theory. But many do not know just how radical or pernicious CRT is — because, as a new study from the American Enterprise Institute shows, the media does not explain its key tenets in its coverage.

How did critical race theory, an obscure concept that had only been discussed in law schools, academic papers, and advanced graduate school courses, suddenly become the *bête noire* of citizens everywhere concerned that their children were being indoctrinated with anti-American nonsense?

The answer lies with the conservative news channel Fox News. As Rashawn Ray and Alexandra Gibbons wrote, also in November of 2021,

> Fox News has mentioned "critical race theory" 1,300 times in less than four months. Why? Because critical race theory (CRT) has become a new bogeyman for people unwilling to acknowledge our country's racist history and how it impacts the present.

Critical race theory is an academic study, until now mostly confined to law schools and graduate programs, where professors and scholars studied how inequities are ingrained and codified in American systems: in the law, in business, and in society. From this starting point, CRT becomes much more intricate and complex. Because of this, its opponents have found it easy to misrepresent and attack it.

To understand the history behind the weaponization of CRT, we must go back a few years to 2020. In that year, a number of high-profile killings of Black men and women were all over the news: Ahmaud Arbery was gunned down for simply jogging in the wrong neighborhood; Breonna Taylor was killed in her bed by police officers who entered the wrong home; and George Floyd was murdered when a police officer, ostensibly subduing a uncooperative criminal, pressed his knee on Floyd's neck for over nine minutes, asphyxiating him. Numerous protests and Black Lives Matter rallies rocked the nation. In response, many schools and organizations instituted sensitivity training around diversity, equity, and inclusion, commonly abbreviated as DEI training.

Conservatives needed a way to fight back. According to the ACLU:

> The conservative activist Christopher Rufo manufactured the frenzy around critical race theory in the government and schools. He reportedly described the fight against critical theory as "the most successful counterattack against BLM [Black Lives Matter] as a political movement." It was never driven by concerns about the best interests of students.

Despite Fox News reports that have led to contentious school board meetings across the country, most people still don't know what CRT is. An anecdote that went viral on the internet offers insight into this confusion. A teacher at a private school was asked by a concerned parent whether she was teaching CRT. The teacher suggested that the parent tell her what CRT was and that, then, the teacher could tell the parent if she was teaching it. The parent was unable to answer.

When Rufo liberated CRT from the dark hallways of academia, he acknowledged the little-known nature of the theory. He wrote: "Relegated for many years to universities and obscure academic journals, over the past decade it has increasingly become the default ideology in our public institutions."

Rufo knew that he could introduce a new term to viewers of conservative media, but given the arcane nature of CRT, he could bend it and shape it any way he wanted. And he did, claiming, "It has been injected into government agencies, public school systems, teacher training programs, and corporate human resources departments in the form of diversity training programs, human resources modules, public policy frameworks, and school curricula."

This was patently untrue. Before 2021, almost no one was discussing CRT at all, except for the aforementioned denizens of ivory towers. But Fox News viewers didn't know that. The result of this manufactured crisis is that Republican lawmakers all over the country have enacted laws to squelch the teaching of CRT in the public schools. It was insignificant that virtually no one in the public schools was teaching it. Conservative media decided that CRT taught two major things to impressionable minds: that white people were responsible for all the challenges faced by Black people, and that they should feel guilty about it. Never mind that this was a gross distortion of the subtle and nuanced ideas around CRT. The strategy worked. Governor Glen Youngkin of Virginia won a term in office by crusading against CRT and for parental rights in education. And teachers all over the United States have been cowed into relative silence on the topic of race by legislation written with a fuzziness that makes educators wonder if they are breaking the law or not.

VIEWPOINT 1

> "Most books being targeted for censorship are books that introduce ideas about diversity or our common humanity, books that teach children to recognize and respect humanity in one another."

Book Banning Targets Minority Authors
Ariana Figureoa

In this viewpoint, Ariana Figureoa writes about how 1,500 books have been banned in public schools. Many of these books are about marginalized populations. One target of such banning is books by Ruby Bridges, a civil rights icon who was the first Black child at an all-white Louisiana school in the 1960s. Many students feel that it is important to hear voices that were traditionally out of the mainstream, but conservative efforts have led to a silencing of these voices. Congressional Republicans have supported these bans, arguing that students can still find banned books in stores or libraries. Ariana Figureoa covers news on Washington, DC, for States Newsroom. Her areas of coverage include politics and policy, lobbying, elections, and campaign finance.

"More than 1,500 books have been banned in public schools, and a U.S. House panel asks why," by Ariana Figureoa, Virginia Mercury, April 8, 2022. Reprinted by permission.

Is There Bias in Educational Curricula?

As you read, consider the following questions:

1. What percentages of banned books have content focused on minority communities, whether about Black or LGBTQ+ individuals?
2. How did Republican congresspersons try to change the subject of banned books during the hearing?
3. Why was a *Maus* by Art Spiegelman, a book about the Holocaust, banned from some schools?

A U.S. House Oversight and Reform Committee panel on Thursday examined why thousands of books, predominantly written by marginalized authors, have been banned from public schools, and the impact of those actions on students and teachers.

"Most books being targeted for censorship are books that introduce ideas about diversity or our common humanity, books that teach children to recognize and respect humanity in one another," said the chair of the Subcommittee on Civil Rights and Civil Liberties, Rep. Jamie Raskin.

Raskin, a Maryland Democrat, cited a new report by PEN America—an organization that advocates for the protection of free speech—that found from July 2021 to the end of March this year, more than 1,500 books were banned in 86 school districts in 26 states.

The report found that of the banned books, 467—or 41 percent —contained main or secondary characters of color; 247, or 22 percent, addressed racism; and 379, or 33 percent, of books contained LGBTQ+ themes.

Raskin held up a children's book that administrators have tried to remove from school libraries. The book was written by Ruby Bridges, a civil rights icon who was the first Black child to desegregate an all-white Louisiana school. Bridges, who was 6 years old at the time, was a witness at the hearing.

"The truth is that rarely do children of color or immigrants see themselves in these textbooks we are forced to use," Bridges

Bias in Education

said. "I write because I want them to understand the contributions their ancestors have made to our great country, whether that contribution was made as slaves or volunteers."

Her book, *This Is Your Time*, is being reviewed for possible removal in a school district in Texas. Books written about her story have been banned in classrooms in Pennsylvania.

High School Students Speak Out

The hearing began with testimony from several high school students.

Olivia Pituch and Christina Ellis, of York, Pennsylvania, said it is important for students to see books written by authors who are people of color, LGBTQ+, Black and Indigenous, and with characters from marginalized groups.

Pituch, who identifies with the LGBTQ+ community, said that if she had been able to have access to books with queer representation, she would have "been able to embrace and love myself a lot earlier on."

"I deserve to walk into my school library and find a book with someone like me," she said.

Ellis, who is Black, said that books that center characters who are people of color also benefit white students, so those students are educated about different cultures.

She talked about how growing up, classmates would make fun of the Caribbean food she brought from home and how her classmates and sometimes teachers would touch her hair.

"Books that highlight our differences, and that teach others how to address diversity, are crucial," she said. "Books can help kids educate themselves on various cultures and ways of life."

Mindy Freeman, a parent from Pennsylvania, said a book called *George (Now Melissa)* was able to help her daughter, in fourth grade at the time, understand what she was going through as a transgender girl. Freeman said her daughter's access to an age-appropriate book provided her the support and visibility she needed.

"No book made my child become transgender any more than a book could have turned her eyes from brown to blue," Freedman said.

Freedom of Speech on Campus

Republicans on the panel, Reps. Jim Jordan of Ohio and Andy Biggs of Arizona, focused on freedom of speech on college campuses, and argued that these places were not welcoming to conservatives.

Biggs asked the Republican witness, Jonathan Pidluzny, what action should be taken so that conservatives are not barred from speaking on college campuses. Pidluzny is the vice president of academic affairs for the American Council of Trustees and Alumni, which is an organization that supports free speech across universities.

"We need to learn to tolerate the speech we abhor," Pidluzny said.

Two Republicans, Reps. Byron Donalds of Florida and ranking member Nancy Mace of South Carolina, asked witnesses about district decisions about school curriculum and school administrators' decisions to ban books.

"Taxpayers should have the ability to review that material because they pay for it," Donalds said.

He, along with Mace, argued that there were other ways that students could get books, such as buying them or going to a public library.

"They can get a book from a lot of different places," Mace said. "Is there anything that prevents a kid from going to a public library?"

Two of the witnesses, Samantha Hull, a librarian from Lancaster County, Pennsylvania, and Jessica Berg, a teacher from Loudoun County, Virginia, said that not every student has the financial means to buy books or has adequate access to transportation to visit public libraries to read books where they see themselves represented.

Berg said that visceral attacks on education from Republicans almost caused her to quit her job. She said she has received death threats from members of her own community as well as continued questioning of her expertise.

"Books ... offer a mirror to readers so they can see themselves reflected in some way, be it their gender, race, culture, identity or experience, and it makes them feel less alone in the world," she said. "When I think about the books frequently being challenged, the only connection I see between them is that they are the books that give voice to the most marginalized in our society."

Mace agreed that history, especially "problematic chapters in our history," should be taught in schools, but said books dealing with adult topics expose young kids to inappropriate topics.

"We should be teaching critical thinking skills," Mace said, adding that she's disturbed by reports of colleges "stifling speech to coddle young adults."

Tennessee Book Banning

Rep. Debbie Wasserman Schultz, a Florida Democrat, held up a graphic novel about the Holocaust that was the latest book to be banned in Tennessee classrooms, *Maus*. She said with the rise in white nationalism, antisemitism and racism, books like *Maus* are now more important than ever.

"We know that bigotry is learned," Wasserman Schultz said, adding that "we also know it can be unlearned."

She asked Hall what removing books like *Maus* and ones that have diverse characters does to students.

"It's my opinion when books are removed ... students are erased," Hall said. "They feel their identities are not valued in the school and outside the school."

Rep. Rashida Tlaib, D-Mich., did not ask any of the witnesses questions but expressed the fear of discrimination her two Muslim sons might face growing up.

"Our children, they just simply want to exist as they are," she said.

VIEWPOINT 2

> "An inclusive curriculum and more stories around sexual minorities during the teaching-learning process could be a starting point for making educational institutions more inclusive of sexual minorities."

A More Inclusive Curriculum Could Target LGBTQ+ Bullying in India

Namrata Shokeen and Shivani Chunekar

Namrata Shokeen and Shivani Chunekar write about the bullying of LGBTQ+ students that occurs in Indian schools. While Indian law has recently decriminalized homosexuality in the country, bullying of students is a continuing issue. Sometimes this bullying has led LGBTQ+ students to commit suicide. Indian schools can do much to alleviate the situation by adopting a more inclusive curriculum, say the authors, one that presents LGBTQ+ people with dignity. Currently, the authors of most Indian textbooks are male, and women and LGBTQ+ voices are not represented. Namrata and Chunekar argue that a more inclusive curriculum and more stories about the LGBTQ+ community during the teaching-learning process would be a good starting point. Namrata Shokeen is a research author in the department of sociology at Monk Prayogshala, a research institute in Mumbai, India. Shivani Chunekar is a junior research assistant in the department of sociology at Monk Prayogshala.

"LGBTQ+ and the Culture of Violence in Education", by Namrata Shokeen and Shivani Chunekar, Psychology Today. Reprinted by Permission.

Bias in Education

As you read, consider the following questions:

1. According to the viewpoint, what are WEIRD countries?
2. How have depictions of gender been a problem in Indian textbooks?
3. According to surveys, what percentage of Indians are LGBTQ+?

In 2018, Indian lawmakers revoked the controversial Section 377 of the Indian Penal Code by decriminalizing homosexuality in the country. However, questions and common-sensical remarks about the non-heterosexual population in India are still often guided by extreme homophobia, social taboo, and a lack of awareness about different sexual orientations. Despite clear-cut statements by the Indian Psychiatric Society that homosexuality is not a mental disorder, one could easily find homophobia lingering around everyday discourses, movies, and popular Youtube videos in India.

It is important to note here that this rejection and denunciation of non-hetero sexualities are not limited to non-WEIRD (non–Western, educated, industrialized, rich, and democratic) countries like India. Social taboo, unacceptance, negative behavior, discrimination, and public shaming are some of the potential reasons for hiding one's sexuality in WEIRD countries like the United States too. As a consequence, the exact population of LGBTQ+ persons is still unknown, and there are substantial variations in the prevalence estimates of the LGBTQ+ population in India as well as the United States.

According to a recent LGBTQ+ Pride global online survey carried out across 27 countries, nearly 3 percent of respondents identified as being homosexual, gay, or lesbian, whereas 4 percent identified as bisexual. In addition, 1 percent identified as pansexual or omnisexual. In India, when asked, "What best describes your sexual orientation," nearly 9 percent identified as bisexual, 3 percent mentioned that they were only attracted to same-sex people, and

17 percent claimed that they were mostly attracted to the same sex. On the other hand, in the United States, nearly 5 percent identified as bisexual, 5 percent said that they were only attracted to same-sex people, and 13 percent claimed that they were mostly attracted to the same sex.

Extreme and Continuing Bullying

Considering the increasing visibility of the LGBTQ+ population in recent years, education becomes one of the most prominent ways of creating awareness and sexual inclusivity among students from a young age. However, various media reports highlight the extreme and continuing bullying against LGBTQ+ persons in the Indian education system (Bhattacharya, 2018; Babbar, 2020). For instance, recently, a young boy from Delhi was continuously bullied and sexually exploited by some boys in his school just because of his effeminate behavior. Despite his multiple complaints to the school faculty, no strict action was taken by the school management, which eventually led him to commit suicide (Mehra, 2022). Furthermore, a 2019 report by UNESCO suggests that 60 percent of LGBTQ+ students face bullying during middle or high school. Forty-three percent have been sexually assaulted, and 33 percent drop out due to continuous bullying in Indian schools.

Stories of bullying, sexual violence, and the continuous trauma due to one's sexuality are again not limited to only non-WEIRD countries. Extensive research suggests that students belonging to the LGBTQ+ population are at a much higher risk of violence than non-LGBTQ+ students in the U.S. education system. The rampant bullying and violence against LGBTQ+ students across the world raises the question of whether schools are aware of the blind spots in terms of sexuality and student safety. Do our schools and education system provide enough training to teachers and students to accept and include a multiplicity of students from different sexual orientations?

However, schooling is essential to how one views the world and where primary socialization takes place. The narratives of

LGBTQ+ students facing harassment, not only by their peers but also by school authorities, tell how important it is to begin to envision what it would be like to have inclusive education. For this, it is important to take stock of how gender and sexuality are taught in schools. Following that, it is also essential to take into account how this impacts children from the LGBTQ+ community.

Gender in Textbooks

Previous research on social studies textbooks shows how the textbook writing staff consists of significantly fewer women than men, which invariably impacts the mention of male and female illustrations and names used in narratives in the textbook. For instance, the study shows that while talking about the Indian freedom struggle, most of the Indian social science textbooks do not illustrate the journey of female freedom fighters, highlighting how they are looked at as secondary rather than an equal part in shaping history

A study on the representation of gender in Indian textbooks further points out how implicit notions are conveyed through the representation of gender in these books, where not only LGBTQ+ students, even women do not find any significant space. The author put forth data on how men and women are represented through occupational status, symbolizing certain traits that reinforce stereotypes of men and women. The existence of such differences and their impact further highlight how patriarchal norms are reinforced through textbooks, in various forms such as illustrations among others. It has an impact on those who read these textbooks as it shapes implicitly how one understands gender roles and identities.

In India, public and private institutions are subject to the University Grants Commission's Anti-Ragging Regulations 2009, which prohibit homosexual assault after the 12th standard. College-level courses follow the Saksham recommendations for gender workshops, but the school system currently is not governed by any rules that help protect students who are marginalized on the basis of their sexuality. The US.. has adopted several state laws and antibullying policies: introducing LGBTQ-inclusive education, passing same-sex civil unions, and allowing transgender people to change their legal gender without any medical or state intervention, protection from discrimination under Title IX in educational amendments. However, a report by GLSEN (the Gay, Lesbian, and Straight Education Network) shows how most of these U.S policies and laws are unable to protect the LGBTQ+ student populations. As a result, many LGBTQ+ students continue to remain prone to victimization, conversion therapies, dropout, poor academic performance, shame, and sexual abuse in both WEIRD and non-WEIRD countries.

Considering the high rates of violence, homophobia, and bias against sexual minorities in the education system, it is time our students as well as school management and teachers are made aware of gender pronouns and the need to respect different sexual minorities. An inclusive curriculum and more stories around sexual minorities during the teaching-learning process could be a starting point for making educational institutions more inclusive of sexual minorities.

VIEWPOINT 3

> "CRT is not, however, a testament to the superiority of Black individuals relative to their white counterparts. Neither is it a political ideology devoid of facts that is meant to spew hate between races and across the nation. In fact, CRT is intended to accomplish the very opposite."

What Critical Race Theory Is, and What It Isn't

Mellissa S. Gordon

In this viewpoint, Mellissa S. Gordon attempts to clarify ideas about critical race theory (CRT), explaining what it is and what it isn't. The concept has nothing to do with Black racial superiority, as some of its antagonists posit. Instead, it looks at the long history of white supremacy and how it has traditionally subordinated people of color. CRT provides a framework for examining how race has played a major factor in the development of this country. Mellissa S. Gordon, Ph.D., is an associate professor in the department of human development and family sciences at the University of Delaware.

"Demystifying Critical Race Theory: What It Is, and What It Isn't," by Mellissa S. Gordon, National Council on Family Relations, September 30, 2021. Shared with the permission of the National Council on Family Relations.

As you read, consider the following questions:

1. Why does Gordon begin the viewpoint by explaining how she identifies?
2. According to Gordon, what are the key tenets of critical race theory?
3. What offshoot movements of CRT have sprung up?

I begin by identifying myself as a Black female scholar who emigrated to the United States from Jamaica at the age of 9. By no means do I proclaim to provide a comprehensive, all-inclusive explanation of a topic as complex as CRT, but I seek to provide the fundamentals of the intentions behind it as a collective movement. Additionally, I outline the basic tenets of CRT for social science research, which have coalesced from the works of people who have contributed at its inception as well as from the works of those who have used CRT to inform their own research, myself included. It is my hope that this piece empowers each of us to advocate for, support, and amplify the voices and experiences of those who are affected by racial inequality.

As interest in CRT has burgeoned recently, misconceptions regarding its intended purpose has also followed suit. Despite the negative proclamations surrounding it, at its core, CRT is a tool that researchers can use when framing work that involves race generally and to provide context to research that highlights racial disparities between the majority and minority populations, more specifically. CRT is not, however, a testament to the superiority of Black individuals relative to their white counterparts. Neither is it a political ideology devoid of facts that is meant to spew hate between races and across the nation. In fact, CRT is intended to accomplish the very opposite (Crenshaw et al., 1995).

Proponents of CRT do not subscribe to an agreed-upon script as to what exactly constitutes critical race scholarship in terms of object of study, argument, accent, or emphasis (Crenshaw et al., 1995). What is agreed on, however, and what has served as the underlying premise of CRT, is the convergence of two shared interests: "to understand how ... white supremacy and its subordination of people of color have been created and maintained in America ... and ... a desire not merely to understand the vexed bond between law and racial power but to change it" (Crenshaw et al., 1995, p. xiii). Whether CRT is considered a movement, a framework, or a scholarship depends on the space in which it is being utilized. More importantly, it encapsulates a formal analysis of how race is conceptualized in direct and subtle ways for the sole purpose of systematically disempowering people of color, exclusively and unjustifiably, on the benign phenotypic expression of the color of one's skin while elevating white constituents (DiAngelo, 2016; Mayr, 2002).

Despite its seemingly exponential growth in popularity, CRT (or some version of it) has been at the forefront of scholarly inquiry for quite some time (Bell, 1980a, 1980b; Crenshaw, 2002; Delgado, 1995). Its "likeness" can be juxtaposed to Bell's (1980a) theory of the interest of convergence, which suggests that "the interest of Blacks in achieving racial equality will be accommodated only when it converges with the interests of whites" (p. 523). To this effect, until white Americans find value in abandoning racism, anti-Black practices by the majority (and anyone for that matter) will be permitted, legitimized, and uncontested.

In recognition of such tendencies, CRT places race at the center of scholarly inquiry. It boldly insists on critical discourse that supersedes a vested interest in maintaining the status quo. To intentionally choose to remain racially unaware, or even worse, being knowledgeable of racial injustices but choosing to remain silent is a detriment to academia generally, and social science scholarship more specifically, as this is likely to remake and replicate existing racial inequities.

Given that CRT is ever evolving and malleable, the following key tenets surmised from the literature are provided as a fundamental base that espouses the need to apply CRT understandings and insights whenever social science research is conducted and/or encountered in policy and practice. The following list is by no means intended to be comprehensive or mutually exclusive:

- Race is socially constructed and complex (Crenshaw et al., 1995).
- Race and racism are institutionalized within systems that seek to maintain racial inequality (Crenshaw et al., 1995; Ladson-Billings & Tate, 1995).
- Anti-racism is not performative. CRT questions claims of neutrality, meritocracy, "color-blindness," and deficit-based research that further denigrates the lived experiences of people of color (Crenshaw, 2002).
- In an effort to counter the permanence of racism, public policy initiatives at the highest levels must be enacted (Crenshaw, 2002).
- CRT is "a product of any scholar [regardless of race] engaged in a critical reflection of race" (Crenshaw, 2002, p. 1363).
- The principles of CRT intersect with the experiences of one or more minoritized group (Annamma et al., 2013; Solórzano & Delgado Bernal, 2001).

CRT provides researchers with a lens in which to frame their work, in a way that acknowledges the role that race plays in shaping their particular findings. Specific to social science research, it has been used to examine how social, political, and economic factors have worked to undermine the normative involvement of Black fathers and family formation patterns over time (Lemmons & Johnson, 2019). Additionally, DePouw (2018) employed CRT to gain a better understanding of the role that whiteness and racial power play in intimate relationships in the family, particularly between White parents and family members of color. Notably, an application of CRT to research does not require the abandonment of neutrality or objectivity (Carbado & Roithmayr, 2014), as some would suggest; nor does it necessitate a plan of action to change the structural dimensions of racism that have, for decades, afflicted American society.

Expansions of Critical Race Theory

While CRT was first conceptualized as an academic framework for examining and understanding how race is constructed and maintained to systematically disenfranchise Black people and elevate the majority group (Crenshaw et al., 1995), its underlying principles have been applied to a number of offshoot movements comprising primarily members of other marginalized populations. For example, Latino CRT (LatCrit) addresses issues concerning the Latino/Latina population in America, such as language, immigration, and acculturation (Solórzano & Delgado Bernal, 2001). Similarly, disability CRT (DisCrit) provides a theoretical framework for exploring the intersectionality of racism and disability. Researchers adapting this perspective are primarily concerned with highlighting the lived experiences of disabled people of color (Annamma et al., 2013). Additionally, quantitative CRT, also referred to as QuantCrit, draws on the tenants of CRT as a means of highlighting the complexities associated with quantifying race in quantitative research. It cautions that numbers are not neutral and are often interpreted in a way that serves the interests of white individuals while promoting the deficits of Black people (Gillborn et al., 2018).

Similar to CRT, the aforementioned offshoot movements seek to broaden our understanding of the complexities of race in influencing every aspect of life in American society, especially among marginalized, underrepresented groups. These expansions propagate the sentiments of the American philosopher and political activist Cornel West, who stated, "Critical race theory is a gasp of emancipatory hope that law can serve liberation rather than domination" (Crenshaw et al., 1995, p. xii). CRT recognizes that racial problems do not simply go away when left unaddressed; even more so, it encourages an acknowledgment of race in shaping U.S. history, *the good and the bad*, not in an effort to stifle our progress toward racial equality but as a means of learning from it, so that the negative aspects of it may not be repeated.

References

Annamma, S. A., Connor, D., & Ferri, B. (2013). Dis/ability critical race studies (DisCrit): Theorizing at the intersections of race and dis/ability. *Race, Ethnicity, and Education, 16*(1), 1–31. https://doi.org/10.1080/13613324.2012.730511

Bell, D. (1980a). *Brown v. Board of Education* and the interest-convergence dilemma. *Harvard Law Review, 93*, 518–533.

Bell, D. (1980b). *Race, racism and American law*. Little, Brown.

Carbado, D. W., & Roithmayr, D. (2014). Critical race theory meets social science. *Annual Review of Law and Social Science, 10*, 149–167. https://doi.org/10.1146/annurev-lawsocsci-110413-030928

Crenshaw, K., Gotanda, N., Peller, G., & Thomas, K. (1995). Introduction. In K. Crenshaw, N. Gotanda, G. Peller, & K. Thomas (Eds.), *Critical race theory: The key writings that formed the movement* (pp. xiii–xxxii). New Press.

Crenshaw, K. W. (2002). The first decade: Critical reflections, or a foot in the closing door. *UCLA Law Review, 49*, 1343–1373.

Delgado, R. (1995). *The Rodrigo chronicles: Conversations about America and race*. New York University Press.

DePouw, C. (2018). Intersectionality and critical race parenting. *International Journal of Qualitative Studies in Education, 31*(1), 55–69. https://doi.org/10.1080/09518398.2017.1379620

DiAngelo, R. (2016). What is race? *Counterpoints, 497*, 97–106. https://www.jstor.org/stable/45157300

Gillborn, D., Warmington, P., & Demack, S. (2018). QuantCrit: Education, policy, "Big Data" and principles for a critical race theory of statistics. *Race Ethnicity and Education, 21*(2), 158–179. https://doi.org/10.1080/13613324.2017.1377417

Ladson-Billings, G., & Tate, W. F. (1995). Toward a critical race theory of education. *Teachers College Record, 97*(1), 47–68.

Lemmons, B. P., & Johnson, W. E. (2019). Game changers: A critical race theory analysis of the economic, social, and political factors impacting Black fatherhood and family formation. *Social work in Public Health, 34*(1), 86–101. https://doi.org/10.1080/19371918.2018.1562406

Mayr, E. (2002). The biology of race and the concept of equality. *Daedalus, 131*(1), 89–94. https://www.jstor.org/stable/20027740

Solórzano, D. G., & Delgado-Bernal, D. (2001). Examining transformational resistance through a critical race and LatCrit theory framework: Chicana and Chicano students in an urban context. *Urban Education, 36*(3), 308–342. https://doi.org/10.1177/0042085901363002

VIEWPOINT 4

> "'This will scare a lot of school districts,' said Columbia, Mo., high school social studies teacher Greg Simmons. 'A lot of teachers don't feel comfortable teaching around race anyway, and this will put a kibosh on all of that.'"

Conservative Lawmakers Aim to Censor School Discussions About Race

Jon Greenberg and Amy Sherman

Jon Greenberg and Amy Sherman discuss how conservative lawmakers are using critical race theory (CRT) to impose a gag order on all discussions of race in the public schools. CRT examines "how a regime of white supremacy and its subordination of people of color have been created and maintained in America." Critics of CRT insist that it paints a negative picture of America, and, in its insistence upon race as a major factor, is racist itself. But supporters of CRT counter that it is merely a toolkit for examining systemic racism in the United States. Republicans have drawn up numerous bills to prohibit the teaching of CRT, but the fact is that critical race theory, in all its nuanced complexity, is not really taught in primary and secondary American schools. What educators feel is that these potential laws will have the practical effect of shutting down all curricula related to race and racial inequities. Jon Greenberg is a

"What is critical race theory, and why are conservatives blocking it?," by Jon Greenberg and Amy Sherman, PolitiFact, May 24, 2021. Reprinted by permission.

senior correspondent with PolitiFact. Amy Sherman is a staff writer with PolitiFact based in South Florida.

As you read, consider the following questions:

1. According to the viewpoint, why isn't CRT "one set thing"?
2. According to Greenberg and Sherman, why do opponents of CRT consider it divisive?
3. What did the executive order by former President Donald Trump prohibit?

Florida Gov. Ron DeSantis, a Republican, is pushing forward on a reworked civics education curriculum for K-12. For DeSantis, the new plan is as much on what it bans, as what it promotes.

"Let me be clear, there's no room in our classrooms for things like critical race theory," DeSantis said at a March press conference in Naples. "Teaching kids to hate their country and to hate each other is not worth one red cent of taxpayer money."

Critical race theory—a broad set of ideas about systemic bias and privilege—might have its roots in legal academia, but it is fast becoming one of the more explosive flashpoints in America's state legislatures.

Conservative lawmakers in over a dozen states, including Missouri, Idaho, and Tennessee, have introduced bills aimed at barring critical race theory in the classroom. The bills generally forbid teachers from offering any instruction that suggests that the United States is fundamentally racist, or that leads students to feel guilty for past actions by white people. Some of the bills expressly use the term "critical race theory" while others ban certain practices.

Educators warn that they will have their intended effect— turning teachers ultra-cautious, confining their lessons to a limited view of American history and current events.

Bias in Education

"This will scare a lot of school districts," said Columbia, Mo., high school social studies teacher Greg Simmons. "A lot of teachers don't feel comfortable teaching around race anyway, and this will put a kibosh on all of that."

Florida state Sen. Shevrin Jones, a South Florida Democrat and former public school teacher, said, "The crazy thing about this is, now critical race theory is not even taught in K-12 education."

Regardless, Republicans are pressing the issue.

What Is Critical Race Theory?

Critical race theory isn't one set thing but more a changing package of ideas.

The grandfather of the movement was Harvard Law School professor Derrick Bell, who in the mid-1970s voiced frustration at the limited impact of landmark civil rights laws and U.S. Supreme Court rulings of the previous decade. While those changes aimed to broaden access to high-quality education, jobs and housing, they fell short, he said. Laws remained embedded in a set of values and practices that discriminated against people of color, Bell said.

Legal scholars, such as Kimberlé Crenshaw, Neil Gotanda, Gary Peller and Kendall Thomas, developed Bell's ideas further. In a 1995 book, they wrote that critical race theory is rooted in the desire "to understand how a regime of white supremacy and its subordination of people of color have been created and maintained in America."

They said that the fundamental problem was the "distribution of political and economic power." And they defined their movement as one that was "race conscious" and was committed to change.

Critics often call the theory Marxist, and there is a tie. As Crenshaw and others wrote in 1995, a "collection on neo-Marxist and new Left activists" in law schools were part of the movement to challenge the ways American law served "to legitimize an oppressive social order." Far from every scholar was a Marxist, so the label is overly broad.

In plain terms, critical race theory holds that racism is part of a broader pattern in America: It is woven into laws, and it shows up in who gets a job interview, the sort of home loans people are offered, how they are treated by police, and other facets of daily life large and small.

What Are the Criticisms of Critical Race Theory?

A central complaint of critical race theory is that, because it focuses on race, the approach is itself racist. Critics say it presents solely a negative picture of the United States and is designed to make students feel badly about their country.

A group of Republican members of Congress introduced a bill and a resolution decrying critical race theory. The lead sponsor, Rep. Burgess Owens, R-Utah, said by focusing on skin color, the theory "preserves" racist thinking and "undermines civil rights."

The head of the Republican Study Committee, Rep. Jim Banks, R-Ind., said, "teaching students to be ashamed of our country and to judge each other based on their race is wrong and divisive." Rep. Rick Allen, R-Ga., added that it "aims to indoctrinate Americans into believing our nation is inherently evil."

Politicians aren't the only ones who are concerned, however. New York University social psychology professor Jonathan Haidt raised a deep concern about the approach's focus on power relationships.

"Every situation is to be analyzed in terms of the bad people acting to preserve their power and privilege over the good people," Haidt wrote. "This is not an education. This is induction into a cult."

Educators who are open to the concepts of critical race theory counter that this is a caricature of what actually goes on inside the classroom. It "is not propaganda or anti-American," wrote professors David DeMatthews and Terri Watson in Education Week.

"It is a toolkit for examining and addressing racism and other forms of marginalization," they wrote.

The ACLU Responds to Florida's Stop W.O.K.E Act

In accordance with Florida's Stop W.O.K.E. Act, which prohibits instruction on systemic racism and sexism, the Florida State Board of Education introduced outrageous African-American history standards that rewrite and whitewash history. These standards require teachers to instruct students that enslaved people developed skills that could be used for their personal benefit, blame enslaved people for violence during massacres, and misrepresent the role of the Founding Fathers in perpetuating slavery.

Judge Mark Walker, who heard the case in the Northern District of Florida, accurately described the Stop W.O.K.E. Act as "positively dystopian" because it limits instruction to the viewpoints approved by the State, regardless of truth.

We Must Continue to Fight

The conservative activist Christopher Rufo manufactured the frenzy around critical race theory in the government and schools. He reportedly described the fight against critical theory as "the most successful

Is It Used in the Classroom, and How Do You Know When It Is?

Opponents of critical race theory suggest that the theory is pervasive, but that's proven hard to pin down.

In Tennessee, press reports said that supporters of a bill to ban critical race theory didn't cite examples from particular schools.

As Arkansas lawmakers debated a similar bill, the focus on local schools fell away, and the bill that passed only restricted state agencies. Arkansas Gov. Asa Hutchinson allowed it to become law without his signature, saying it "does not address any problem that exists."

Elements of a race-conscious approach can appear in education policies, but not as part of a full package of critical race theory.

> counterattack against B[lack] L[ives] M[atter] as a political movement.'"
> It was never driven by concerns about the best interests of students.
>
> The fight to regain or protect the status quo has obscured meaningful discussions about what was missing from education all along: the narratives and experiences of BIPOC and LGBTQ+ people and women.
>
> Over the past two years, I've watched attacks on education morph from demands to exclude critical race theory from classrooms to even more dangerous demands to erase entire concepts from American history. Book bans, so-called transparency laws designed to intimidate educators into compliance and attacks on individual expression have left our education system at the mercy of a hostile and discriminatory minority. Students can't learn in that type of environment.
>
> Our future depends on educational institutions that value instruction about systemic racism and sexism. We need to expand culturally relevant instruction and increase funding for diversity, equity, and inclusion in schools, not attack it for its role in uplifting the systematically oppressed. We can't afford to lose our education system as we know it. We must fight back.
>
> "What the Fight Against Classroom Censorship Is Really About," by Leah Watson, ACLU, September 7, 2023.

The Illinois' State Board of Education has guidelines for teachers that say they should "understand that systems in our society create and reinforce inequities," and "be aware of the effects of power and privilege." Those ideas fit under the broad umbrella of critical race theory, but they would fit just as well under any approach to social studies that applied a realistic lens to current problems in America.

University of Missouri education professor LaGarrett King said the problem is blown out of proportion.

"The majority of teachers are not even familiar with what critical race theory is, nor do they teach it in their classrooms," King said.

King and his colleagues have worked on study plans to help high school teachers get at tough issues, including slavery and economic inequality. None mention critical race theory itself, but some draw on the idea of systemic racism.

"It's a lens, but it's just one of the things taught in that class," King said. "It doesn't define the whole curriculum."

Does It Say White People Should Feel Guilty?

One target of critical race theory opponents is the *New York Times'* 1619 Project. In 2019, the newspaper published a series of articles on race and the legacy of slavery in America. 1619 refers to the year when the first enslaved Africans were brought to Virginia, then an English colony. The opening essay by Nikole Hannah-Jones includes this passage:

> "The United States is a nation founded on both an ideal and a lie. Our Declaration of Independence, approved on July 4, 1776, proclaims that 'all men are created equal' and 'endowed by their Creator with certain unalienable rights.' But the white men who drafted those words did not believe them to be true for the hundreds of thousands of black people in their midst."

The 1619 Project is critical of school portrayals of slavery and offers lesson plans for teaching about it in school.

Missouri Rep. Brian Seitz, a Republican, singled out this effort in his bill to bar critical race theory in schools.

"I think critical race theory, and in particular the 1619 Project, does in fact seek to make children feel guilt and even anguish, not because of anything they've done, but solely based on the color of their skin," Seitz said May 3.

Emotional responses depend on the person, but there's no intent to make anyone feel guilty, said Columbia, Mo., high school history teacher Simmons.

Simmons draws his students at Battle High School into researching uncomfortable topics, such as issues raised by the Black Lives Matter movement. Simmons said he can't control how someone might react, but he doesn't frame things in terms of guilt. And he uses his own education as an example.

"We need to be real with students and show them the complexities of the world," Simmons said. "I grew up in rural Missouri in a family that used the N-word. When I got to college, I took some history and Black studies classes. Those things opened my eyes to a world that I had no clue about. My instructor didn't try to make me feel guilty. I took it as, things are messed up. Is there some way we can make them less messed up?"

That problem-solving approach changed the fate of a Utah bill. A measure to ban critical race theory in that state's schools was moving forward until Republican Gov. Spencer Cox blocked it. Cox said he was no fan of critical race theory, but he had another concern.

"The difficulty, however, comes in defining terms and making sure that we are never stifling thought or expression—and that we make sure our children learn both the best of our past as well as our mistakes so we don't repeat them," Cox said May 17.

What Are States Doing?

Lawmakers in about a dozen states have introduced bills that target teaching that might be considered part of critical race theory. The details vary.

Some bills, like the ones in Idaho and Missouri, mention critical race theory by name. Others don't, but they all share the approach—as in Tennessee, Arizona and Iowa—of listing prohibited practices.

Those lists draw from—often word for word—the items in a September 2020 executive order from former President Donald Trump. Trump aimed to ban federal workplace training that touched on systemic racism. Trump's list, for example, barred anything that said:

- "The United States is fundamentally racist or sexist."
- "An individual, by virtue of his or her race or sex, is inherently racist, sexist, or oppressive, whether consciously or unconsciously."

Bias in Education

- "Any individual should feel discomfort, guilt, anguish, or any other form of psychological distress on account of his or her race or sex."
- "Meritocracy or traits such as a hard work ethic are racist or sexist, or were created by a particular race to oppress another race."

To avoid charges of squelching free thought, many of the bills, such as Louisiana's, say that nothing in the bill should prevent teaching about "divisive topics." Some specifically protect discussion of race and discrimination.

In Florida, DeSantis said he banned critical race theory, but it wasn't a part of the curriculum previously. Rather, the state's new draft civics curriculum emphasizes teaching about patriotism and love of country, citizenship, the U.S. form of government, and the Constitution. A proposed rule bans teachers from indoctrinating students with information beyond the state's standards. State education commissioner Richard Corcoran said in a recent speech that the state is keeping "crazy liberal stuff" out of Florida's schools.

That has fueled criticism of DeSantis and the draft curriculum. Ted Thornhill, director of the Center for Center for Critical Race and Ethnic Studies, wrote in an op-ed that the comments by DeSantis were "dangerous, calculated race-baiting nonsense."

Simmons, the Missouri high school teacher, says what seems lost in the debate is the good that can come from discussing hard topics like race.

"I was raised to be racist and sexist," Simmons said. "That's a bias that I had to work through. The kids I teach see the world differently. And they are much more accepting of anyone who is different in any way. They get it."

Periodical and Internet Sources Bibliography

The following articles have been selected to supplement the diverse views presented in this chapter.

Michael E. Dantley, "Racist Curricula in the 21st Century Do Exist," American Association of Colleges for Teacher Education, https://aacte.org/2019/12/racist-curricula-in-the-21st-century-do-exist/.

Louise Derman-Sparks and Julie Olsen Edwards, "Understanding Anti-Bias Education: Bringing the Four Core Goals to Every Facet of Your Curriculum," *Young Children,* November 2019. https://www.naeyc.org/resources/pubs/yc/nov2019/understanding-anti-bias.

Wayne D'Orio, "Truth in Textbooks: Unpacking Bias in Curriculum Staples," *School Library Journal*, November 26, 2019. https://www.slj.com/story/Truth-in-Textbooks-Unpacking-bias-in-curriculum-staples-libraries.

Anthony Izaguirre and Adriana Gomez Licon, "'Don't Say Gay' law brings worry, confusion to Florida schools," PBS, August 15, 2022. https://www.pbs.org/newshour/education/dont-say-gay-law-brings-worry-confusion-to-florida-schools.

Sandra Jones, "The Right Wing Is 'Whitewashing' History Curriculum Taught in Public Schools," *Bucks County Beacon*, February 21, 2023. https://buckscountybeacon.com/2023/02/the-right-wing-is-whitewashing-history-curriculum-taught-in-public-schools/

Rashawn Ray and Alexandra Gibbons, "Why are states banning critical race theory?," Brookings, November 2021. https://www.brookings.edu/articles/why-are-states-banning-critical-race-theory/.

Christopher F. Rufo, "Critical Race Theory: What It Is and How to Fight It," *Imprimis*, March 2021. https://imprimis.hillsdale.edu/critical-race-theory-fight/.

David Sadker, "Some Practical Ideas for Confronting Curricular Bias," Myra Sadker Foundation. https://www.sadker.org/curricularbias.html.

Stephen Sawchuk, "What's Driving the Push to Restrict Schools on LGBTQ Issues?," *Education Week*. April 19, 2022. https://www.

edweek.org/leadership/whats-driving-the-push-to-restrict-schools-on-lgbtq-issues/2022/04.

J.D. Tuccille, "Biased Textbooks Are Just Part of the Public School Curriculum Wars," *Reason Magazine,* January 30, 2020. https://reason.com/2020/01/30/biased-textbooks-are-just-part-of-the-public-school-curriculum-wars/.

Michael R. Wenger, "The Dangers of Teaching Whitewashed American History," American Association of Colleges and Universities, January 21, 2021. https://www.aacu.org/liberaleducation/articles/the-dangers-of-teaching-whitewashed-american-history.

Zachary B. Wolf, "What the bill dubbed 'Don't Say Gay' by critics actually says," CNN, March 28, 2022. https://www.cnn.com/2022/03/10/politics/florida-dont-say-gay-bill-what-matters/index.html.

For Further Discussion

Chapter 1

1. After reading the viewpoints in this chapter, do you think that teacher bias often affects how teachers grade student work? If so, what kinds of biases?
2. After reading the viewpoint by Peter Tymms, are you convinced that teachers favor students who share their personality traits? Why or why not? How might it impact how teachers act, according to this viewpoint?
3. After reading the viewpoint by Jason Pohl, do you believe that school discipline is administered fairly? Explain your reasoning.

Chapter 2

1. After reading the viewpoints in this chapter, do you believe that the college admissions process is a fair one? Why or why not?
2. After reading the viewpoint by Matt Bruenig, do you think that college admissions (as well as other school admissions) are impacted by economic class? Explain your answer.
3. After reading the viewpoint from the Pew Research Center, do you believe that race should be a factor in school admissions? Why or why not?

Chapter 3

1. After reading the viewpoints in this chapter, do you feel that politicians have too much power over education, too little, or just enough? Explain your reasoning.
2. From what you've read, do you think the political divide in the U.S. has a negative effect on teaching and learning in classrooms? Why or why not?

Bias in Education

3. Do you agree or disagree with Tim Walker when he argues that all education is political? Explain your reasoning.

Chapter 4

1. "We need to learn to tolerate the speech we abhor," says Republican Jonathan Pidluzny in the viewpoint by Ariana Figureoa. Do you believe this should be a goal of education? Why or why nto?
2. After reading the viewpoint by Namrata Shokeen and Shivani Chunekar, how do you think the representation of different genders in textbooks impacts attitudes toward women and LGBTQ+ people?
3. After reading the viewpoints by Mellissa S. Gordon and Jon Greenberg and Amy Sherman, what do you think critical race theory is? In your experience, is it currently being taught in schools? Explain your answer.

Organizations to Contact

The editors have compiled the following list of organizations concerned with the issues debated in this book. The descriptions are derived from materials provided by the organizations. All have publications or information available for interested readers. The list was compiled on the date of publication of the present volume; the information provided here may change. Be aware that many organizations take several weeks or longer to respond to inquiries, so allow as much time as possible.

American Civil Liberties Union (ACLU)
125 Broad Street
New York, NY 10004
(212) 549-2500
website: www.aclu.org

The ACLU is one of the nation's leading guardians of liberty, working in courts, legislatures, and communities to defend and preserve the individual rights and liberties that the Constitution and the laws of the United States guarantee. Among the issues it focuses on are human rights, racial equality, and women's rights.

American Enterprise Institute for Public Policy Research (AEI)
American Enterprise Institute
1789 Massachusetts Avenue, NW
Washington, DC 20036
(202) 862-5800
email: tyler.castle@aei.org
website: www.aei.org

The American Enterprise Institute is a conservative public policy think tank that sponsors original research on the world economy,

U.S. foreign policy and international security, and domestic political and social issues. AEI is dedicated to defending human dignity, expanding human potential, and building a freer and safer world. Their scholars and staff advance ideas rooted in their belief in democracy and free enterprise.

The Association of American Educators (AAE)

25909 Pala, Suite 330
Mission Viejo, CA 92691
(800) 704-7799
website: www.aaeteachers.org

The Association of American Educators (AAE) is the largest national, non-union, professional educators' organization. It advances the profession by offering a modern approach to teacher representation and educational advocacy, as well as promoting professionalism, collaboration, and excellence without a partisan agenda.

Cato Institute

1000 Massachusetts Avenue NW
Washington, DC 20001
(202) 842-0200
website: www.cato.org

The Cato Institute is a libertarian public policy research organization and a think tank dedicated to the principles of individual liberty, limited government, free markets, and peace. Its scholars and analysts conduct independent research on a wide range of policy issues.

Center for American Progress (*CAP*)

Address: 1333 H Street NW, 10th Floor
Washington, DC 20005
(202) 682-1611
website: www.americanprogress.org

The Center for American Progress is a public policy research and advocacy organization which presents a liberal viewpoint on economic and social issues. Their website includes a range of articles on various social issues.

The Heritage Foundation
214 Massachusetts Ave NE
Washington DC 20002
(800) 546-2843
email: info@heritage.org
website: www.heritage.org

The Heritage Foundation is a conservative think tank. The organization's mission is to formulate and promote conservative public policies based on the principles of free enterprise, limited government, individual freedom, traditional American values, and a strong national defense.

The National Association for the Education of Young Children (NAEYC)
1401 H Street NW
Suite 600
Washington, DC 20005
(202) 232-8777
website: www.naeyc.org

The National Association for the Education of Young Children (NAEYC) is a professional membership organization that works to promote high-quality early learning for all young children, birth through age eight, by connecting early childhood practice, policy, and research. They advance a diverse, dynamic early childhood profession and support all who care for, educate, and work on behalf of young children.

Bibliography of Books

Tracey A. Benson and Sarah E. Fiarman. *Unconscious Bias in Schools: A Developmental Approach to Exploring Race and Racism*. Cambridge, MA: Harvard Education Press, 2019.

Linda F. Bisson, Laura Grindstaff, Lisceth Brazil-Cruz, and Sophie J. Barbu, eds. *Uprooting Bias in the Academy: Lessons from the Field*. Springer: Cham, Switzerland, 2022.

Theresa Marie Bouley and Anni K. Reinking. *Implicit Bias: An Educator's Guide to the Language of Microaggressions*. Lanham, MD: Rowman & Littlefield, 2021.

J. Scott Carter and Cameron D. Lippard. *The Death of Affirmative Action?: Racialized Framing and the Fight Against Racial Preference in College Admissions*. Bristol, UK: Bristol University Press, 2020.

Louise Derman-Sparks, Julie Olsen Edwards, and Catherine M. Goins. *Anti-Bias Education for Young Children and Ourselves*. Washington, DC: National Association for the Education of Young Children, 2020.

Michael H. Gavin. *The New White Nationalism in Politics and Higher Education: The Nostalgia Spectrum*. Lanham, MD: Lexington Books, 2023.

Henry A. Giroux. *Race, Politics, and Pandemic Pedagogy: Education in a Time of Crisis*. London, UK: Bloomsbury Academic, 2021.

Gina Gullo, Kelly Capatosto, and Cheryl Staats. *Implicit Bias in Schools: A Practitioner's Guide*. New York, NY: Routledge, 2019.

Frederick M. Hess and Pedro A. Noguera. *A Search for Common Ground: Conversations About the Toughest Questions in K-12 Education*. New York, NY: Teachers College Press, 2021.

Bibliography of Books

Stafford Hood, Henry T. Frierson, Rodney K. Hopson, and Keena Arbuthnot, eds. *Race and Culturally Responsive Inquiry in Education: Improving Research, Evaluation, and Assessment.* Cambridge, MA: Harvard Education Press, 2022.

Matthew Kincaid. *Freedom Teaching: Overcoming Racism in Education to Create Classrooms Where All Students Succeed.* Hoboken, NJ: Jossey-Bass, 2024.

New York Times Editorial Staff. *Affirmative Action: Still Necessary or Unfair Advantage?* New York, NY: New York Times Educational Publishing, 2021.

Hedreich Nichols. *Finding Your Blind Spots: 8 Guiding Principles for Overcoming Implicit Bias in Teaching.* Bloomington, IN: Solution Tree Press, 2022

Jessica Nordell. *The End of Bias, a Beginning: The Science and Practice of Overcoming Unconscious Bias.* New York, NY: Metropolitan Books, 2021.

Joel Spring. *American Education* (Sociocultural, Political, and Historical Studies in Education). 20th ed. New York, NY: Routledge, 2024.

Melvin Urofsky. *The Affirmative Action Puzzle: A Living History from Reconstruction to Today.* New York, NY: Pantheon Books, 2020.

Index

A

affirmative action, 50, 71–72, 78–80, 85–89, 118, 122

American College Testing (ACT), 34, 50, 55, 59–63, 65–68, 71, 74

B

Black Lives Matter (BLM), 14, 133, 155, 158

brain drain, 108–111

C

censorship, 135–139, 155

colleges and universities, 14, 16, 28, 50–52, 54–57, 59–91, 96–107, 114, 117–123, 127, 132–133

COVID pandemic, 52–53, 58, 63, 67, 72, 74–75, 115, 117, 119

critical race theory (CRT), 120, 132–134, 146–150, 152–160

D

disability, 30, 36, 55, 57, 150

E

elementary schools, 14, 27, 55, 152–153

empathy, 28–29, 45, 78–79

eugenics, 54, 56–57

explicit bias, 15–16, 18–19, 30

extracurriculars, 51, 64–65, 81–83

G

gender, 15–16, 30, 35, 37, 41, 59, 62, 64, 79, 97, 119, 126, 139, 141, 143–144

GPA, 63, 65–69, 76

H

high schools, 14, 16, 18, 26, 34, 45, 55, 57, 64–68, 71–72, 75–76, 79, 105, 137, 152–153, 157–158

I

implicit bias, 15–16, 18–19, 25–26, 28–38

Ivy League, 51, 81–82, 84

L

legacy admissions, 71–73, 82–83, 104

Index

LGBTQ+ issues, 18–19, 36, 96, 120, 135–137, 141–145, 155

P

politics, 14–15, 86–88, 91, 96–107, 111, 113–128, 132–135, 138–139, 153
poverty, 20, 59, 61–62, 71, 77
private schools, 58, 76–77, 114

R

racism, 28, 33, 35, 37, 52–53, 56, 59, 62, 70, 72, 75, 124–127, 132–133, 136, 139, 147–150, 152–157, 159–160
religion, 30, 36, 70, 126

S

Scholastic Aptitude Test (SAT), 50, 55–56, 59–68, 71, 74, 103
1619 Project, 158
standardized testing, 50, 52–72, 74–75, 81–84
STEM, 15–16
stereotypes, 15, 28, 30–31, 34–35, 40
Supreme Court, 19, 77–78, 117–118, 122, 154

Index

Index